God is preparing you for a
bright and blessed future!
–Joel

Your Future Is in God's Hands

JOEL OSTEEN

Your Future Is in God's Hands

Printed in China

ISBN 978-1-951701-35-2

Created and assembled for Joel Osteen Ministries by
Breakfast for Seven
2150 E. Continental Blvd., Southlake, TX 76092
breakfastforseven.com

Contents

Introduction

What if the key to your success wasn't in time management techniques, to-do lists, or rethinking your priorities? What if the key to making the most of your time and discovering God's plan for your life was about trusting His timing and being faithful in the waiting?

Jeremiah 29:11 says, *"'For I know the plans I have for you,' declares the LORD, 'plans to prosper you and not to harm you, plans to give you hope and a future'"* (NIV). The plans that God has for you are good. In fact, they are great. But God isn't in a hurry to give you the blueprints to your destiny. He is not impatient for you to get started.

God has a plan for your life, for your future. It is a plan that is beyond your wildest imagination. It is a good plan, a grand plan — a plan that He has been preparing and paving for you. He has been storing up blessings, waiting for the right time for those blessings to burst forth. But He is the One who sees the big picture, not you.

He sees how much time you need to develop the maturity necessary to handle a God-sized blessing. He sees who else plays a role in your destiny and how much time they need. He is so precise; He knows the exact day, the exact hour that His plan will become manifest in your life. He won't be one second late, but He also won't be one minute early. Your future would look very different if He was.

"Your future is in God's hands" should be the most reassuring statement that you have ever read. But if you've got control issues (like most of us), if you are impatient (like most of us), if you have a hard time rejoicing when others get blessed before you (like most of us), then this statement is probably a challenge; and you definitely need to read this book!

You will learn the importance of not only trusting God and His plan for your life, but also trusting His timing. He wants to knock your socks off with the plans He has for you. They are plans you can't even dream up. What is the wildest dream for your life? God's future for you is wilder! Do you dream of writing a book? God wants it to be a bestseller! Do you dream of meeting new friends? God wants them to become your best friends. Do you dream of getting a raise? God wants to double your salary! But because God loves you so much, He's not going to give you that dream until you are ready for it. Only He knows when that time is, when you can handle it, and when it will be the biggest blessing to you. He wants your future to be full of bright blessings and fulfilled dreams.

The question is, can you enjoy the wait? Can you keep your peace in the growing seasons? Can you trust God when nothing seems to be happening, when it is taking longer than you expected, when it feels like He has all but forgotten the promise He gave to you and your future seems uncertain? Can you believe that when He isn't answering you, it's because He has a greater miracle in store?

As you read through these pages, declare the promises of God over your life: "God has a plan for my life. His plan for me is good, not evil. His plan is to prosper me and not to harm me. His plan for me is a hope-filled life. His plan is exceeding abundantly above and beyond my wildest imagination. My future is in His hands!"

I pray that you will take hold of these promises and learn to relax and enjoy life even while you wait for your future to unfold. Miracles are in store. Resurrections are in store. Abundance is in store. Healing and restoration are in store. But there is no reason you shouldn't enjoy life just as it is right now while He is preparing you for a blessing-filled future. When you truly trust that He has a good plan for you, when you truly let go and put your future in His hands, you can enjoy every season of your life!

Waiting Well

The Time Has Already Been Set

In life, we're always waiting for something: waiting for a dream to come to pass, waiting to meet the right person, waiting for a problem to turn around. When it's not happening as fast as we would like, it's easy to get frustrated. But you have to realize the moment you prayed, God established a set time to bring the promise to pass.

God has a set time for you to meet the right person. There is a set time for the problem to turn around, a set time for your healing, your promotion, your breakthrough. It may be tomorrow, or next week, or five years from now. But when you understand the time has already been set, it takes all the pressure off. You won't live worried, wondering when this is ever going to happen. You'll relax and enjoy your life, knowing that the promise has already been scheduled by the Creator of the universe.

Some of you have been praying about a situation for a long time. You don't see anything happening. You could easily be discouraged. But what if God were to pull back the curtain and allow you to see into the future, and you knew that on February 12, at 2:33 in the afternoon, you were going to meet the person of your dreams? You wouldn't be discouraged. You would be excited. You would start working out. You would go buy some new clothes. You would make the most of this season. Why? You know the big day is coming.

Here's where it takes faith. God promises that there are set times in our future, but He doesn't tell us when they will be. Your set time may be tomorrow morning at 9:47. You'll get the phone call you've been waiting for. Your set time may be October 25, two years from now. You'll get a good break that will thrust you to a new level.

My question is, "Do you trust God enough to believe that your set times are coming?" Are you willing to wait with a good attitude, knowing that they're on their way?

It says in Hebrews, *"For only we who believe can enter his rest"* (Hebrews 4:3, NLT). The way you know you're really believing is you can rest. You're at peace. You know the answer is on the way. You know the right people, the right opportunities have already been set in your future.

What you're praying about, what you're believing for — it's not going to be one second late.

On January 8, 1986, at four o'clock in the afternoon, I walked into a jewelry store to buy a battery for my watch. Out walked the most beautiful girl I had ever seen. It was Victoria. I didn't tell her, but I thought, "This is my set time." (It took me a year to convince her that it was her set time too.)

On December 3, 2003, at one-thirty in the afternoon, when Mayor Brown handed us the keys to the Compaq Center, that was not an ordinary time. That was a set time ordained by the Most High God.

What am I saying? You can trust God's timing. God has it all figured out. What you're praying about, what you're believing for — it's not going to be one second late. If it hasn't happened yet, it doesn't mean something is wrong. It doesn't mean God is mad at you. It doesn't mean it's never going to work out. God has already established the time, down to the split second. You don't have to worry. You don't have to live frustrated. When you know the time has been set, you'll have peace. Whether it's 20 minutes or 20 years, you know what God promised, He will bring to pass.

It would be a lot easier if God told us when we were going to get well, when we would meet the right person, when our child would straighten up. But the truth is, that wouldn't take any faith. It takes faith to have peace in the waiting periods. It takes faith to believe that our set times have already been established. It takes faith to wait well.

Declaration

God, I'm going to make the most of my time. I don't know when You are going to answer my prayers, but I trust You enough to believe that You will and that the answer is already in my future. I declare that I will have peace while I wait for my set time to come.

Waiting the Right Way

We're all going to wait, but it's important to learn to wait the right way. The right way to wait is to wait in faith, wait with expectancy, wait with praise, thanking God in advance that what you are waiting for is on the way.

When Abraham was 80 years old, and his wife Sarah was 70, God gave them a promise that they would have a baby. God said in Genesis 18:14, "*Is anything too hard for the LORD? I will return to you at the appointed time next year, and Sarah will have a son*" (NIV).

God said, in effect, "You think it's too late for you, you don't see how it can happen; but I have already set the right time." She will give birth "*at the appointed time.*" Notice God set the time *when He gave the promise.* Whatever God has promised you, He's already set the right time. It's already in your future. The question is, what will you do while you wait?

Wait the right way. Live with a "right time mentality."

God's timing is not our timing. On the way to your promise being fulfilled, there will be opportunities to get discouraged, to give up on what you're believing for, to wait the "wrong way." That's when you have to dig down deep and say, "God, I trust You. I know You wouldn't have promised me this if you didn't have a right time on my schedule." Don't live with an "It's never going to happen" mentality. Wait the right way. Live with a "right time mentality."

Romans 4:19–21 says:

> *Without becoming weak in faith [Abraham]*
> *considered his own body, now as good as dead*
> *[for producing children] since he was about*
> *a hundred years old, and [he considered] the*
> *deadness of Sarah's womb. But he did not doubt*
> *or waver in unbelief concerning the promise*
> *of God, but he grew strong and empowered*

*by faith, giving glory to God, being fully
convinced that God had the power to do what
He had promised.* (AMP)

Abraham did not doubt or waver. He knew that
in the flesh he was "*as good as dead*," but in the
spiritual realm, he was just getting started. Instead of living sour, wondering, "God, when is it
going to happen? We're too old; it's been too long,"
he believed that their right time was coming. He
believed that, because God said it, He would do it.
He believed that he would one day hold the child
of promise in his arms.

I can hear Abraham, all through the day, saying,
"Lord, thank You that the right time is coming. We
don't see how, we don't know when, but we do know
You are a faithful God. We know that when You
promised us the child; You put the right time on our
schedule. You already know the birthday of our son."

Genesis 21:2 says, "*Sarah became pregnant and
bore a son to Abraham in his old age, at the very time
God had promised him*" (NIV). God doesn't give
you a promise without setting the right time. He
puts it on the calendar. But how we wait is up to us.

We can wait discouraged: "When is it going to
happen? Is it going to happen? Why would you
tease me like this, God?"

Or we can switch over into faith. Like Abraham, we can be empowered by faith, "*fully convinced*" that if God said it, it will come to pass at the right time.

Be a believer and not a doubter: "*But as for me and my house, we will serve the LORD*" (Joshua 24:15, NKJV). My child may be off course, but I thank You that the right time is coming. God, You said You'd make me the happy mother of children. I haven't been able to conceive yet, but I thank You that the right time is coming. God, You said You would prosper me in a famine. I may be starving now, but increase, promotion, abundance are already scheduled for me." When you understand that God is going to make it happen, it takes the pressure off. You can relax. You can live in peace. You can wait in faith. You can praise Him while you wait.

Declaration

God, I'm going to make the most of my time by waiting the right way. Until my set time comes, I'm going to wait well, wait in peace, wait with unwavering belief that what You promised will come to pass at my set time.

Be Faithful in the Waiting Period

Many of you know my story, that I became the pastor of Lakewood after my father unexpectedly passed away. But you may not know about all the years behind the scenes that led up to the day I preached my first sermon.

After I graduated from high school, I went to Oral Roberts University to study radio and television, then came back to Lakewood and started the television ministry for my father. I worked behind the scenes, doing the production. I loved putting my father's messages on television. I loved all the editing, the lighting, the live television specials. My father was very supportive at first, but toward the end of his life, he didn't want to do it anymore.

One time, I lined up all these radio stations to air my father's broadcast. It had taken us months to get everything worked out. I was just about to sign the agreements when my father said, "Joel, I'm 75 years old. I'm not looking for any more work. I don't want to make those radio programs. I just want to relax and pastor the church."

What He has in store is going to be bigger than what you have in mind.

I was so disappointed. I thought, "God, I'm young. You've put these big dreams in my heart. I don't want to do less; I want to do more." It was like God was saying, "Not yet. Joel, be patient. You're in a waiting period, but your season is coming." I didn't understand it. I knew I had more in me. I thought, "Maybe it's time to move on and work for someone else." I had an offer from another large ministry, but when I got quiet and listened to that still small voice, I knew I was supposed to stay. I told my wife, Victoria, "This is my father's vision. He's been here for almost 40 years. I'm not going to get sour because I'm not getting my way. I'm going to honor my father and do what he wants to do."

I made the decision to be my best in the waiting period — to do the right thing even when I didn't feel like it. I never dreamed that two years later my father would go to be with the Lord, and I would be the pastor. I realize now God put those dreams in my heart for my own ministry, not for my father's ministry. Things weren't happening before because it just wasn't the right time. Had I not passed those tests and been faithful in the waiting period, I don't think I would be where I am today.

God knows what He's doing. If He's asking you to wait, that means what He has in store is going to be bigger than what you have in mind. Is God saying "not yet" to you in some area? Are you praying for something to change, but it's not happening? Are you believing for a dream, hoping for a break-through, but nothing is any different? Be faith-ful. You're in a waiting period. Keep doing the right thing.

Matthew 11:28 says, "*Learn the unforced rhythms of grace*" (MSG). *Unforced* means you don't have to struggle. You don't have to fight against everything you don't like. You don't have to force a dream to come to pass. You can relax. You can live "freely and lightly" at rest, knowing that God is unfolding

His plan. It may not be happening on your timetable, but God knows when the right time is.

If you're not making progress now, there's nothing wrong. It's just not the right time. Instead of living uptight, come in to the *"unforced rhythms of grace."* Quit worrying, quit being frustrated; your times are in His hands. The God who created the universe is going to unfold His plan for your life.

Psalm 37:4 says, *"Delight yourself in the LORD, and he will give you the desires of your heart"* (ESV). It doesn't say you'll have to work for it, earn it, make it happen. It says God is going to give it to you. It's going to happen without the struggle, without the frustration, without the experience. It's going to be easier than you think — if you'll be faithful in the waiting period.

Declaration

God, I'm going to make the most of my time by waiting faithfully. I know that if it hasn't come to pass yet, it's because You have something better in mind. I'm not going to force it. I'm going to be my best in the waiting period.

Don't Lose Your Cows

When I was growing up, my father would have a big conference at our church every Thanksgiving. It was one of the highlights of the year. He would bring in hundreds of missionaries that we support from around the world.

At one conference, he decided he wanted to feed everyone at Lakewood. Months before the conference, he prayed and asked God to give him two cows; that way he would have enough meat for all the people. He believed he received it when he prayed, but week after week went by, and there was no sign of any cows. He kept believing, telling the church the cows were on the way; but every thought said, "You're wasting your time. Nobody has ever given you a cow. Maybe you should have prayed for something easier, smaller, like chickens." As the time got closer, thoughts whispered, "You have the money; just buy the cows. It's not going to happen; just buy the cows." My father finally got worn down. He quit talking about the cows and went out and bought the meat for the conference.

Weeks after the conference was over, he had a dream. He saw in this dream a huge snake out in a field. Inside that snake, he could see the distinct outline of two cows. He woke up and God said to him, "I just want you to know you let the enemy have your two cows." Those cows already belonged to my father. In the unseen world, they were on the way. But when we quit believing, when we get discouraged, we lose our cows.

Determine to never stop believing that He who promised is faithful, and what you have prayed for is already yours.

I wonder how God would have answered that prayer. I wonder who would have given my dad the cows — a rancher, a grocery store, a slaughterhouse, or someone that would have just shown up in worship one day. I wonder about the miracle he missed because he gave in to the pressure of the enemy telling him it wasn't going to happen.

What have you missed out on — what cows have you lost — because you stopped believing? Determine to never lose your cows again! Determine to never let the thoughts of the enemy overshadow what God has promised you. Determine to never stop believing that He who promised is faithful, and what you have prayed for is already yours.

You may have missed out on some cows like my father did, but don't let that stop you from believing for the next ones. I believe that was a valuable lesson for my father — one that he never forgot and one that he never repeated. From that day forward, he determined to never lose his cows again. He determined to wait in faith, believing that the promise would come to pass in God's way and God's timing.

Waiting seasons reveal our faith while trying our patience. They reveal how much we trust God and if we believe the promises He has placed in our spirits. Waiting well means knowing that what you received in your spirit is en route. You will get well. You will get out of debt. You will achieve your dreams. You will meet the right person. You will get the job. You will overcome addiction. You will see your children follow Jesus. You will! It's just a matter of time before your cows show up.

Hebrews 10:23 says, "*Let us hold fast the profession of our faith without wavering; (for he is faithful that promised;)*" (KJV). Hold fast your profession, keep believing, keep thanking God, keep talking like it's coming. Keep believing that your cows are on the way!

God is faithful. Don't let the lack of evidence convince you that nothing is happening. In the unseen realm, things are changing in your favor. Stay in faith. It's just a matter of time and you're going to see what God promised come to pass. I believe and declare what you received in your spirit is about to show up in the natural. Get ready for promotion, healing, breakthroughs, freedom, the right people, vindication, the fullness of your destiny, in Jesus name.

Declaration

God, I'm going to make the most of my time by holding fast my profession. I believe that what You put in my spirit You are faithful to bring it about. I will keep believing that what You promised is on its way. Thank You for the blessings that are already mine!

When No One Is Watching

God has blessings that are going to chase you down and increase that's going to come looking for you. David was a teenager, out in the shepherd's fields, when Samuel came looking for him. David wasn't seeking fame, power, or notoriety; he was seeking God. Out in the shepherd's fields, he was making the most of his time by being his best when no one was watching.

David was determined to be the best shepherd he could be, honoring his father and having fun skipping rocks in his free time. None of the conditions said, "You're about to be anointed king." He wasn't being celebrated, he didn't have a glamorous resume, no one was putting in a good word for him. All the circumstances said that an ordinary shepherd's life was his destiny. Until one day there was a knock at David's father's door. The prophet Samuel came to Jesse's house to anoint David as king.

I wonder if you are about to receive a knock: if Samuel is about to show up at your house; if you're about to receive an unexpected phone call, a divine connection, a good break that takes you from the background to the foreground. It will be something you didn't see coming but is a direct result of who you have been when no one (but God!) has been watching.

"Joel, I don't think this could happen. Not now. Not for me." God does things out of the ordinary. When it doesn't seem likely, when you don't have the connections, when things have slowed down, get ready for a knock on the door. Get ready for something unusual. "Well, Joel, you're just getting people's hopes up." You can't have faith if you don't first have hope! If you don't want your part, God will give it to someone else.

Why don't you step up to who you were created to be? You're a King's son, a King's daughter! David said in Psalm 27:13, "[What, what would have become of me] had I not believed that I would see the Lord's goodness in the land of the living!" (AMPC).

I'm asking you to believe that you are about to see the goodness of the Lord, believe that favor is on your life, and believe that something good is going to happen to you.

Samuel came to David — the least likely one — the youngest son out in the shepherd's field. His was an insignificant position, but because he was faithful when no one was watching, that one knock on the door changed David's life forever. After he was anointed, he went back to the shepherd's field but now it was different. When he saw Goliath, he picked up a rock and put it in his sling and brought down the mightiest Philistine warrior. He became an overnight hero. When it's your time to shine, you will defeat big enemies with small resources. You don't have to have great talent, great influence, or great experience because when you have God's favor, you will bring down great giants and great obstacles; you and God are a majority.

The scripture says David was a man after God's own heart (1 Samuel 13:14). He wasn't perfect — he made mistakes; but he had a desire to honor God, even when no one was looking. When God can trust you, when He knows He can count on you to honor Him to handle the influence and the resources the right way, then there's no limit to where God will take you. You don't have to be perfect; we all make mistakes. It's not so much about your performance, but it's about your heart. It's about your motives. It's about what you do when no one is watching.

You're not just anyone — you're a King's son, a King's daughter. Know who you are!

Keep God in first place. Do the right thing when it's hard. Say no to things that are pulling you down. Be your best, especially when no one is watching. You're not just anyone — you're a King's son, a King's daughter. Know who you are!

Opportunity is about to knock on your door. Make sure it finds you being your best, doing your best, pursuing God, and honoring Him.

Declaration
God, I'm going to make the most of my time by being my best even when no one is watching. I am going to pursue You with my whole heart even if my life feels ordinary right now, because I know that I'm about to receive a holy knock!

In Season and Out of Season

Psalm 1:2 says to meditate on God's Word day and night. When a person does this, it says in verse 3, *"That person is like a tree planted by streams of water, which yields its fruit in season and whose leaf does not wither—whatever they do prospers"* (NIV). Notice that it doesn't say they will bring forth fruit 365 days a year. It says, they will bring forth fruit "in season." If there is an "in season," that means there is an "out season."

I have lemon trees in my backyard. They don't produce lemons all year long, but they have a season where they're full of lemons. We fill four or five large buckets full of lemons when they are in season. But at certain times of the year, there's no growth, no blossoms, no fruit. The lemons are "out of season." They aren't ripe. The conditions aren't right. If those lemon trees could talk, do you think they would be saying, "What's wrong with us? We don't have any lemons! We've lost our touch. God has forgotten about us." I don't think so. I think those lemon trees would be just as calm and peaceful as they could be — not the least bit worried. Why? Because they know there's nothing wrong; they're just not in season.

Maybe you're in a stuck season — a dry period where you are not seeing any growth. What if, like those lemon trees, there's nothing wrong. It's just timing. You're in a waiting period, a developing period; but when you come in to your season, you will bring forth much fruit!

The question is, when you're not in a producing season, a growing season, a harvest season, are you going to get discouraged and think it's never going to change? Are you going to lose your passion and give up on what God promised you? Or are you going to meditate on God's Word day and night, keeping your mind filled with thoughts of hope and faith? When you do that, remember, when the time is right, you're going to come into your season where whatever you do will prosper.

My lemon trees don't have to work to produce lemons. They don't have to struggle and put forth all this effort to do the thing they were created to do. When they're in season, it happens automatically; it's who they are. In the same way, when you come into your season, you're not going to struggle, you're not going to have to make things happen, and you're going to naturally bear fruit.

Don't get discouraged when things aren't happening as fast as you would like.

God is going to cause the right people to find you. Gifts are going to come out that you didn't know you had. Good breaks are going to track you down. You may have been waiting for a long time, you're tempted to get discouraged, but get ready! You're about to come into your season. You're going to see new growth, unexpected favor, and blessings that catapult you to the next level. You couldn't have made it happen on your own, but because you've been faithful in the waiting periods, because you've done the right thing in the slow times, God is going to bring you into the harvest season — the abundance season.

Don't get discouraged when things aren't happening as fast as you would like. Remember: every season is not a growing season; every season is not harvest. There are seasons of watering, seasons of planting, seasons of pulling up the weeds and fertilizing the ground and simply waiting. These are important seasons. They are times of testing where God is seeing what we're made of. These are seasons of preparation, seasons of rest, seasons of renewal.

When we try to force things to happen out of season, we will frustrate ourselves unnecessarily. But when we wait for the right season to come, we will bear much fruit. We will experience abundance and prosperity with grace and ease.

Declaration

God, I'm going to make the most of my time by meditating on Your Word day and night, because I know that when I do that, I am preparing for my "in season." Right now I may be out of season, but this is the time when I get to rest in Your presence and feed on Your Word. My in season is coming, and I will bring forth much fruit!

When God Says "Not Yet"

None of us like to wait. When we are forced to wait, it is easy to get frustrated and think, "God, if You are going to give me the desires of my heart in six months, or in two years, why don't You do it now? Why don't You bring the right person now? Why don't You give me the promotion now?"

God knows what He's doing. Most of us know that intellectually, but if we are living frustrated, worried, and impatient, we aren't living as if it is true. The truth is, if God promoted you before you were ready, it wouldn't be a blessing; it would be a burden. You wouldn't be able to handle it. He has to get you prepared for what He has in store. He loves you too much to let it happen too soon. You may have a promise in your heart — you know God has given it to you — but you don't see anything happening. God is using the waiting period to do a work in you. If you'll pass the test, if you'll have faith and patience, then you're growing, your character is developing, and your spiritual muscles are getting stronger.

"Joel, my friends are being promoted but not me. I don't understand it. I come to church every week; they only come on Easter." Don't compare your situation with somebody else's. You're not running their race. God may be taking you to a higher level than they will ever reach. It's going to require more character, more discipline, and more commitment. Keep doing the right thing. Your time is coming.

When our son Jonathan was ten years old, I didn't give him the car keys and say, "Jonathan, go take a drive. I want you to have everything that I have stored up for you." I didn't let him have the car, not because I wanted to keep things from him, limit his life, or make him miserable. I didn't do it because I loved him. I knew him having a car at ten wouldn't have been a blessing, it would have been a curse. Sometimes God shows His love for us not by what He gives us but by what He withholds. If He would have let you marry that first man that you wanted to marry, you wouldn't be here now. If He would have let you have that promotion, that job, that house, that baby before you were ready, it would have limited your future. He knows what we can handle, so sometimes in order to protect us, He'll say, "not yet." Don't fight it. Don't just trust God, trust His timing. "Not yet" doesn't mean it's never going to happen. It means it's not the right time. Jonathan has a car now. He just had to grow up. It was a part of the process.

A good father may have a good gift, but he won't give it at the wrong time.

God not only knows what you're going to need, but He knows who you're going to need. Another reason God might be saying "not yet" is because somebody else who is going to be involved in your story is not ready. He's still working on them. They're going to be instrumental in your life, they're going to open a door, they're going to be a close friend, or they're going to be your spouse, or your mother-in-law. God needs time to get them prepared. Be patient, and go through the waiting period with a good attitude.

James 1:17 says, "*Every good and perfect gift is from above, coming down from the Father of the heavenly lights, who does not change like shifting shadows*" (NIV). A good father may have a good gift, but he won't give it at the wrong time. God is a not a good Father; He's a great Father, and He has perfect gifts in store for you — more than you can ask or think. Don't be frustrated if He's not giving it to you yet. Keep growing, keep being good to people, keep passing the tests. God can see the big picture. He knows what you're going to need. You may think you're ready, but you can't see how high God is going to take you. When it's taking longer, that means God has something bigger than you think.

Declaration

God, I'm going to make the most of my time by embracing Your "not yet." I not only trust You, but I trust Your timing. I know that when You say "not yet," it's because You have something so big in store for me that it requires extra planning.

Wait for the
Plan to Unfold

Psalm 106:13, says, *"But they soon forgot what he had done and did not wait for his plan to unfold"* (NIV). What you're believing for may be taking longer than you thought. You're not making progress; you're not seeing dreams come to pass, but God knows what He's doing. Don't try to force things to happen. Don't forget what He has done for you in the past. Wait for His plan to unfold!

This is what Joseph did. You can read his story in Genesis 37–50. He was picked on by his older brothers, tossed in a pit, and sold into slavery. He was falsely accused and forgotten in jail. He had every reason to feel sorry for himself, yet he kept passing the tests in the waiting seasons. When it wasn't fair, when he was betrayed, when he was falsely imprisoned, he kept believing in God and waiting for His plan to unfold.

When Joseph was just 17 years old, God told him that he would be in a position of power, that his brothers and even his father would one day bow down to him. But it took decades for that plan to unfold. Joseph was 30 before Pharoah put him in charge of Egypt — thirteen years of God ordering his steps in a way that he would never have expected or chosen.

Had Joseph not gone through those tests with the right attitude and developed his character and proved to God he could handle being in leadership, then he would have never been put in a position of power. You can have great faith, and you can believe for big things, but without patience to wait for the plan to unfold, you'll get stuck. Going through the waiting periods without a good attitude will limit your destiny.

While Joseph was in the pits, he had every reason to say, "God, where did You go? Look at what's happening to me!" You're not going to understand everything that happens. You may be in a difficult place. It doesn't look like it's ever going to change. Stay in faith; your steps are ordered. You're right on schedule. That delay, the detour, the disappointment are all part of God's plan. If you'll be patient and wait for that plan to unfold, then like Joseph, you're going to come out increased, promoted to a new level of your destiny. When you make the most of your time by waiting patiently for the plan to unfold, you'll go from the pits to the palace; and it will be so good, it will make up for all that you endured in your waiting season.

Everything that you are going through right now is all part of the unfolding of God's plan.

What has God done for you in the past? What promise has He made over your future? What is the thing that you are believing for?

Everything that you are going through right now is all part of the unfolding of God's plan. Rise to the challenge. Don't become bitter; become better. Trust each step that He places in front of you on the journey. Continue to remind yourself of all the good He has done for you in the past. You have survived 100 percent of your bad days, and you'll not only survive this one too, but it will lead you to your destiny.

After Joseph was put in charge of Egypt, it would still be several more years before his dream was fully realized. He had all the power. He had wives and children. Yet something was still missing. Who knows that you can seemingly have it all and yet still not be walking in the fullness of God's purpose and plan for your life? Keep the faith! The plan is still unfolding. Joseph was in power for seven years of abundance, but it wasn't until after those seven years when Egypt entered into seven years of famine that Joseph would be reunited with his family, and he would fully realize his destiny to save his people.

When all is said and done and God's purpose for your life is finally revealed, you will be so glad that you waited for His plan to unfold. Don't miss God's best for you. It is worth the wait.

Declaration

God, I'm going to make the most of my time by waiting patiently for Your plan to unfold. I will trust the process. I will remember what You have done. I will keep the right attitude as Your plan for my life unfolds.

Don't Just Trust God; Trust His Timing

Several places in the Scriptures say, "There is an appointed time for the promise to be fulfilled." "An appointed time" means a right time; and if there's a right time, that means any other time is the wrong time. If you don't understand that God will always be right on time, then the delays, the detours, the waiting periods will frustrate you. But you can't receive the promise out of God's timing. It's not enough to just trust God; you have to trust His timing.

Read that again: It's not enough to just trust God; you have to trust His timing.

He knows when you're ready. He knows when it's the right person. He knows when to open the door, when to turn it around. If it's not happening yet, then you have to be mature enough to accept that it's not the right time. Instead of living upset, when you trust God's timing, you can say, "God, my times are in Your hands. You know when to bless me, when to promote me, when to deliver me. It hasn't happened yet, so I know it's not the right time. God, I trust You, and I trust Your timing."

Hebrews 6:12, says, "... *imitate those who through faith and patience inherit what has been promised*" (NIV). Notice that it says faith AND patience. It's easy to have faith; it's easy to believe for your dreams, but faith without patience will get you into trouble.

God is working behind the scenes. You may not be able to see it, but the right time is coming.

Just ask Moses. As a young man, Moses knew he was supposed to deliver the Israelites. He had the promise, but he didn't have the patience. He got in a hurry and killed a man who was mistreating a Hebrew slave. Moses' heart was right, but his timing was off. Even the right motives at the wrong time just won't work. Moses had to flee for his life and ended up spending 40 years as a shepherd for his uncle, all because he got out of God's timing. If Moses were here, he would tell you it's good to have faith but make sure you have patience. It could save you 40 years of waiting!

You don't have to promote yourself and manipulate people and convince them to like you. We should be persistent and determined, but you don't have to beat down a door. At the right time, things will fall into place; at the right time, the right people will show up; at the right time, the problem will turn around. Now, do your part and wait for the right time. You're not falling behind; you're not being left out. You're right on schedule. God is working behind the scenes. You may not be able to see it, but the right time is coming. God is arranging the right people; He's lining up the right breaks; He's ordering your steps.

You'll know it was the hand of God because you didn't have to force the door to open; you didn't have to play up to people. You came into your time, and God made things happen that you couldn't make happen.

When Moses went back to Egypt to save his people, God not only opened the door for Moses to lead the Israelites out of slavery, but He caused everyone to open their purse strings and the Israelites went out rich (see Exodus 12:35–36). That's what it is to have God's favor and His timing.

I know you trust God, but I'm asking you to trust His timing. Keep a good attitude even when you're not making progress. Do the right thing even when you're not seeing growth. Have faith AND patience; your right time is coming.

One more lesson from Moses: just because you've passed the waiting test once doesn't mean you'll never have to pass it again. Moses had to wait 40 years to return to Egypt, but then he had another 40 years of wandering the desert before he would see the Promised Land. Don't just trust God; trust His timing!

Declaration

God, I'm going to make the most of my time by having faith AND patience. I trust You, AND I trust Your timing. I know that if there is a right time, there is a wrong time; and I'm waiting for it to be right! I know that You will bring me to the right place at the right time, and that will be the appointed time for Your promise to be fulfilled.

Right-on-Time God

One Sunday when my father was alive, I was up in the television control area on the second floor of our church. The service was about to start. I remembered something I needed to tell my father, so I ran down the stairs. As I was running down the curved staircase, I locked eyes with a man who was walking through the lobby. He looked at me and said, "My cousin has a construction permit for a full power television station here in Houston. I'd like to talk to you about it." He handed me his card. It was a ten second conversation, if that. Long story short, we bought the permit and put the station on the air. A few years later, we sold it for a significant profit. Those funds were instrumental in us renovating our building.

Opportunity will find you; blessings will chase you down. He's a right-on-time God.

Notice how precise God is. If I would have been running down the stairs five seconds later, I would have missed him. If I would have stopped to say hello to someone, or if he would have left his house a minute earlier, or if I had remembered in the first place the thing that I had to tell my father, we wouldn't have been there at the same time. Our paths wouldn't have crossed. But God ordered our steps down to the second, "You be at this place, you be at that place," and suddenly we came into our season. God makes things happen that we could never make happen. Right now, God is not only ordering your steps, but He's ordering the steps of the people you need. He's going to cause your paths to cross. Opportunity will find you; blessings will chase you down. He's a right-on-time God.

In the Scripture, when God did something significant, many times it says it happened "suddenly," "immediately," "at once." There wasn't any sign of things to come, of breakthroughs, of chance encounters that would propel them to their destiny. Nothing looked any different, and all of a sudden, things changed. God was showing us He can turn things around without any warning. He can increase you when you don't see any sign of it happening. It's unexpected, out of the blue. You were just doing the right thing, going through the difficulty with trust in your heart, not complaining, not saying, "When is this ever going to change"; then suddenly you came into your season. Suddenly your business took off. Suddenly your health turned around. Sometimes things happen gradually — you can look back and see the progression, the unfolding; but other times it is suddenly and all at once. One touch of God's favor will thrust you to a new level. When you understand God has some "suddenlies" for you, then even when it's taking a long time, you'll still have an expectancy knowing that any minute your suddenly could show up. One phone call, one good break, meeting one right person, and you'll come out of the waiting period into your season of blessing.

Just as God orders steps into times of testing, or times of proving, He orders steps into seasons of favor, seasons of increase. Trust me: your season is coming. You're about to see a suddenly; you're going to come into a season of much fruit — a season of growth, where God thrusts you to a new level. He's going to put you at the right place at the right time. He's not going to send you to a general area at a generic time, "Somewhere over there will do. Any time in the next week or two will do." No, God is not random. He is not vague. He is precise. He is detailed. He is specific, down to the split second, the exact millimeter. He is a right-time-right-place God!

Quit being frustrated because it's not happening as fast as you would like. Be faithful. Be patient. You're right on schedule, your steps are being ordered. It's just a matter of time before you "suddenly" see what God has been doing behind the scenes for you.

Declaration

God, I'm going to make the most of my time by waiting well, with faith and patience, believing that You have some "suddenlies" lined up for me when promises will come to pass, dreams will be fulfilled, problems will turn around, and the fullness of my destiny will be revealed, in Jesus' name.

Delight yourself also in the Lord, And He shall give you the desires of your heart.

Psalm 37:4, NKJV

Sun, Stand Still

Philippians 4:7 talks about a peace that is beyond human comprehension. Have you ever experienced that peace? The odds are against you. Victory seems impossible. You are facing a crisis that seems insurmountable, and yet you have peace.

After Moses died, Joshua was left in charge of leading the Israelites into the Promised Land and staking their claim. This meant a constant battle against the neighboring cities. One time, Joshua and the Israelites were battling five armies at once. God told Joshua that he was going to win, but the problem was they were running out of time. It was about to get dark, and the enemy forces would have the opportunity to escape. They could regroup and come against Joshua and his army again in the morning.

Joshua needed more time. Instead of being discouraged, thinking it was too late, Joshua kept his peace. He looked up in the sky and boldly said, *"Sun, stand still over Gibeon; Moon, stop over Aijalon Valley"* (Joshua 10:12, GNT). I can imagine people looking at Joshua thinking, "Are you crazy? Who are you to think you can stop time? You are outnumbered. You can't just pause the solar system and think you can win this battle. But the scripture says, *"So the sun stood still and the moon stayed in place until the nation of Israel had defeated its enemies"* (v. 13, NLT).

You're not running out of time; time is on your side because God is on your side.

God is not limited by a clock, by a calendar, by your age, or by the year. This is your change to step up to a new level — your chance to break that addiction, to go back to school, to make your marriage great. You're not running out of time; time is on your side because God is on your side. God is going to cause you to accomplish more in less time. He's going to make you more effective, more productive, more focused, and more skilled. There's going to be great favor on your life.

Don't sit back and think, "I waited too long, I'm too old. I don't have the experience, the training, the discipline." Instead, like with Joshua, God is going to freeze time. He's going to give you the opportunity to finish what you started.

I once met a lady who was 103 years old. Her mind was as sharp as can be. She had a great sense of humor. She told me how she'd promised her mother that she would get her college degree, but she got married and spent years raising her children. Then she worked an office job; and after retirement, she was busy with her grandchildren. In the back of her mind, it always bothered her that she didn't keep her promise to her mother. She kept putting it off. In her nineties, she started having some health issues. After spending a couple months in the hospital, it didn't look like she was going to make it, but somehow she recovered. When she was released, she told the doctor that she was going to college to get her degree. She spent three years getting her degree, and at 103, she was the oldest person to ever graduate from that university. God knows how to freeze things until you accomplish what He put in your heart.

It may feel like you're running out of time, but God wouldn't have given you a destiny and then not given you the time to fulfill it. It may seem like it's too late, you've missed your season, if you would have pursued that dream 20 years ago it would have worked; or if you would have invested in your marriage, your business, your children back then, then you could have accomplished it. No there's still time. Do like Joshua and say, "Sun, stand still. God, I need more time to spend with my children, to finish my education, to accomplish my dream." God gave Joshua an extra day to finish his assignment. You're not running out of time. Time is on your side. I believe and declare that everything God has put in your heart will come to pass.

Declaration
God, when the odds are against me, I will stay in peace, believing that time is on my side. Freeze time for me; make the sun stand still until I have defeated my enemies and accomplished my dreams. It is not too late!

It's Just a Matter of Time

We all have things we're believing will change. We're fighting an illness; we're struggling with an addiction; we're dealing with fear, anxiety, or depression. We know what God promised — that He would restore our health, that our children would serve the Lord, that we would be free from the fear. We prayed, we believed, but we don't see anything improving. What you can't see, however, is that the moment you prayed in the unseen realm, the source of what was coming against you — fear, addiction, sickness, etc. — was cut off. Now, you may not see any manifestation for some time. There may not be any evidence that anything changed, but this is where many people get discouraged. There will always be a time period where it looks like God isn't going to do what He promised. The fear still comes, the medical report hasn't improved, the addiction is just the same. But what's feeding those things has been cut off. It looks like they're still alive, but the truth is the fear is dead, the addiction is dead, the trouble at work is dead. Don't get discouraged because you don't see anything happening. It's just a matter of time. What God promised you is on the way.

The Gospel of Mark tells of a day when Jesus was leaving Bethany and saw a fig tree with leaves on it off in the distance. Leaves meant figs, and Jesus was hungry, so He went out of His way to go to the tree. However, when He got closer, He discovered that the tree didn't have any figs after all. Jesus said to the tree, "*May no one ever eat fruit from you again*" (Mark 11:14, NIV).

The disciples watched, waiting for the tree to shrivel up and die, but the tree was still just as healthy and full of leaves as before. I can hear the disciples whispering, "It didn't work this time. What happened? Did He lose His power?" They had seen Jesus speak to a blind man and heal his eyes. They had heard him speak to the sea and calm the water, but this time when He spoke, nothing changed. There was no evidence that what He said had happened.

Don't get discouraged because there are still leaves on the tree. Don't lose your peace when the thing you've prayed about doesn't look any different. All the power that's trying to stop you is being cut off. It may be hindering you now, but it's only temporary. It's not going to last. It's lost its source. Every day it's withering, every day it's getting weaker. On the outside it may look the same, but on the inside, it is drying up.

The next day, the disciples passed by that same tree; but this time, "*they saw the fig tree withered from the roots*" (v. 20). When Jesus spoke to the tree, nothing happened on the outside, but on the inside, down in the roots, the source was cut off. When the roots are dead, the tree is dead. It may still look alive, it may still have green leaves, it may still have wide branches; it looks like it's healthy and strong. But it's just a matter of time before the outside catches up with the inside.

When Jesus spoke to the fig tree, there was no sign that anything happened; but this is what faith is all about. You can't be moved by what you don't see; you have to be moved by what you know. What we know is that if God said it, He will do it. And what He said was, "*I will break the strength of the wicked, but I will increase the power of the godly*" (Psalm 75:10, NLT). Do your part and stay in faith until what you are praying for manifests. Keep believing that the strength of that thing holding you back has been broken. Keep thanking God, keep talking like you're free, keep thinking like you're healthy, keep acting like you're victorious. It's just a matter of time before the outside catches up.

Declaration

God, I declare that I am free. I have prayed against the things that bind me, and You have cut them off at the root — at the source. Even though I can't see it yet, I will keep trusting in You until the thing I'm praying for is made manifest. In Jesus' name, Amen.

Blossoms and Breakthroughs

Hebrews 12:3 warns us: do not "*faint in your minds*" (KJV). When God is taking His time giving you His promises, the first place we lose the battle is in our thinking. Thoughts will tell you, "You've been struggling for years. If God wanted you to overcome this, you would have by now." Don't believe those lies. What's trying to stop you is temporary. Soon, things will change in your favor.

We have some friends who send us a dozen roses every Easter. They come in a box. They have long stems, with a rose bud on the top. What's interesting is, even though the rose is dead, even though it's been cut off from the bush, when you put that stem in water, the rose will bloom. It's dead, but it will still blossom. It has no life, but it will still get bigger, expand, and increase.

Stay encouraged. It may bloom, or it may blossom, but it's still dead. It's just a matter of time before it withers up and fades away. All through the day, you can say, "Father, thank You that the source of this trouble has been cut off. Thank You that You cursed the roots of this fear, You spoke to this addiction, You commanded this sickness to wither and die. Lord, I stay in agreement with You."

When we were trying to acquire the Compaq Center, we had a lot of opposition. After a couple of years, we finally got enough council members to be for us, and we won the vote. We were so excited. We knew God gave us the victory. But three days later a company that owns all the property around the building filed a federal lawsuit to try to keep us from moving in. They were the largest taxpayers in Texas — a big real estate company. We thought the opposition was over, but it was just beginning. It was just starting to bloom. I was tempted to worry, "God, what are we going to do? We don't have a chance!" But instead, I had to do what I'm asking you to. I said, "God, I will not faint in my mind. I believe the strength of those coming against us has been cut off. They're bigger, they're stronger; but

I know You being for us is more than the world being against us."

Like that rose bud that blooms even though it's dead, don't be surprised if you have opposition that blossoms, adversity that blooms, giants that try to stop you. They look like they have the upper hand. Stay in peace, their source has been cut off. What you're up against is only temporary. It's just a matter of time before you see the hand of God. When all the odds were against us and it looked like this building could be tied up in the courts for years, we were told that the other side would never back down. But one day out of the blue, they called and said they wanted to meet. We met with them, they agreed to not only let us have the building but to lease us 9,000 covered parking spaces. That two-year legal battle suddenly came to an end.

You're about to see some of these suddenlies. You believe that the roots have been cut off of the things that you've been praying about, but it seems like it's still alive. Get ready because that addiction is about to suddenly go, that depression is about to suddenly stop, that opposition is about to suddenly be defeated, that sickness is about to suddenly change. It may be blossoming now, but that's a sign it's on the way out! That's a sign that you're close to your breakthrough. You're close to a new level. You're close to freedom like you've never seen.

God, I will not faint in my mind. I will hold on
to the truth: that You are good, that You do good,
and You have a good plan for my life. When trouble blossoms, I know I am headed for my breakthrough! Freedom is on the way.

All Bark
and No Bite

I've heard it said that the enemy makes the most noise when he's on the way out.

One morning, after a rocky night of fishing, Jesus got out of the boat with his disciples and was immediately approached by a demon-possessed man who lived amongst the burial caves. Mark 5 says, *"When Jesus was still some distance away, the man saw him, ran to meet him, and bowed low before him. With a shriek, he screamed, 'Why are you interfering with me, Jesus, Son of the Most High God? In the name of God, I beg you, don't torture me!' For Jesus had already said to the spirit, 'Come out of the man, you evil spirit'"* (vv. 6–8, NLT).

When Jesus told demons to come out of people, often they would let out a loud scream — a *"shriek"* as the above passage describes it. They would cause all kinds of noise and commotion. Not because they were getting stronger, however, but as a sign that they were leaving — they were being cast out.

The Scripture says, *"Your enemy the devil prowls around like a roaring lion looking for someone to devour"* (1 Peter 5:8, NIV). He's not a lion, but he sure sounds like one sometimes. He'll make a lot of noise, he'll talk a lot of trash, but his bark doesn't match his bite.

There is a story of a lady who had a dream. In this dream, she was in her house and an evil looking person came in and started taking her possessions. She watched from the second floor over the banister as he put her things in a large bag. In the dream, she began to pray, saying, "In the name of Jesus I have authority over you. Leave my things alone." The man mocked her and said, "I'm not afraid of you or your prayers." He continued through the house taking her things. She said it again, "You have to go." He'd laugh and say, "I don't have to leave. Your prayers won't stop me; you don't have any authority over me." But she noticed while he was saying this, he started putting all her things back. He kept mocking her, laughing, causing a great commotion, but at the same time he was returning everything he took. This went on until he had put everything back in its proper place. Eventually he went running out of the house, but she could still hear him all down the street saying, "I'm not afraid of you, you have no authority over me."

All the time that the enemy is making a commotion, getting loud and stirring up trouble, what he won't tell you is he's putting everything back. Like the story of the woman and her dream, the enemy will talk a big talk, he'll get louder and louder; but all the while, he is actually losing strength. He's throwing his voice. He's moving farther away. He's untying the knots he had around your finances, your health, your children, your freedom. He's putting your salary back. He's putting your test scores back. He's putting your health back. He's putting your family back. He may be louder, but he's on his way out. He makes the most commotion when he's about to leave.

You can speak words of power in Jesus' name.

Sometimes when we pray, it doesn't seem like anything is happening. It's like the enemy is laughing, mocking us, saying, "You're not free from this addiction, you'll never get well, your kids will never get back on track." That's when you have to remember: he makes the most noise when he's on the way out. It's in those moments that you have to stay in faith, keep praying and keep believing, and remember that he is all bark and no bite!

Don't panic when things get worse. What you thought was dead will come back to life. God is still on the throne. He has authority over the enemy, and you can speak words of power in Jesus' name. He has the final say.

Declaration

God, I refuse to be afraid of the enemy's chatter. When he gets louder, I will take that as a sign that he is on his way out. When life gets harder, I will double down in faith and believe that victory is right around the corner. I am at peace because I know I am headed for a breakthrough.

Not One Day, but "Today"

Jesus said in Mark 11:24, *"Therefore I tell you, whatever you ask for in prayer, believe that you have received it, and it will be yours"* (NIV). It doesn't say, believe it when you see it. It doesn't say, believe you are healthy when your test results show improvement. It doesn't say, believe your finances have turned around after you have a nice nest egg. It says, pray first, believe second, and receive third. This means you believe when you prayed that your healing came. You believe when you prayed that your finances turned around. You have to receive it in your spirit before it's going to happen in the natural. You have to be healed in your spirit before you'll see healing in your body. You have to be prosperous in your spirit before you'll be prosperous in the bank account.

Too often we believe that we're *going to* receive it: "One day I'm *going to* get well, one day my children are *going to* do right, one day I'm *going to* break this addiction." That is *going to* limit us. The prayer of faith says, "When I pray according to God's Word, I believe it happens *right when I pray*. I have it in my spirit. It's already mine." If you don't receive it in your spirit first, then you won't see it in the natural. Don't say "one day"; declare that it is yours *today!*

When my mother was diagnosed with terminal cancer, she and my father prayed for healing on December 11, 1981. That day my mother believed she received her healing. She had just been given a few weeks to live. Her skin was yellow, and she weighed only 89 pounds. Nothing in the natural said she was healed. But that day she not only prayed but she believed that she received the healing. For months nothing looked any different, she didn't feel any better. It looked like that cancer was winning, but she kept saying, "Father thank You that on December 11 when we prayed, I received my healing. I believe that day the tide of the battle turned in my health." She kept thanking God, she kept calling herself well, she kept declaring scriptures over her life. "I will live and not die, with long life God satisfies me." She started getting better and better. Eventually she was completely well. The healing she received in her spirit when she wasn't well, eventually showed up in her physical body.

When you believe you receive when you pray, then you don't keep asking God to do it. You start thanking Him because it is already done. If you've already received your healing, then you don't have to ask for healing again. You don't have to keep begging God, "Please heal me." Instead, start saying, "Father thank You that I am healed. Thank You that I am blessed."

Maybe you're believing for a scholarship. "Father, I'm asking you for this scholarship and I believe that I receive it right now. I believe it happened." You receive it by faith. From now on you pray, "Father thank You for the scholarship." You just keep thanking God, keep talking like it's already happened. You may not see anything changing. Every voice says it's never going to work out. That's when you have to dig down deep and say, "It's mine *today!*"

There are forces constantly trying to convince us that what God said is never going to happen: "It's been too long, there's no sign of it, it would have happened by now. Just accept that it's not going to work out." Don't believe those lies. In the unseen realm, things have already changed. Not one day, but "today." The miracle is already in motion. It's just a matter of time before the manifestation shows up. Don't get talked out of it. Don't give in to the temptation to let it go. Don't give up on your dream, your healing, your child, or your freedom. It's closer than you think. Today is your day!

Declaration

God, I am not going to give up on what You promised me. I'm not going to let negative thoughts talk me out of it. I prayed, I believed, and I know that what I received in my spirit is on the way in the natural. Thank You for blessing me, not one day but "today!"

Perfect Timing

James 1:2–4 says, "*My brethren, count it all joy when you fall into various trials, knowing that the testing of your faith produces patience. But let patience have its perfect work, that you may be perfect and complete, lacking nothing*" (NKJV).

We live in a society that not only doesn't want to struggle or go through trials, but one that also wants everything *right now*. We are being programmed for immediacy. *Don't make me wait!* But the Scripture says that we are incomplete without patience. Our faith is immature without the tests and the trials and the waiting periods that produce good fruit.

It's obvious that God wants us to have faith, but it should be equally obvious that He wants us to have patience. Begin to pray like this: "God, I not only believe for big things, but I trust Your timing. I'm not going to get discouraged if it doesn't happen immediately. I'm not going to give up because it's taken a week, a month, or five years. I know the set time is already in my future, so I'm going to wait with faith and patience because I know that it's on the way."

When Victoria was pregnant with our first son, Jonathan, the first few months were very exciting. There were no problems at all. But about six months in, Victoria started getting uncomfortable. Her feet started swelling. By the seventh month, her back was hurting. She couldn't sleep at night. By the eighth month, she was saying, "God, I want to have this baby *right now*. I am tired of waiting!" But we knew God had an appointed time. The child was not ready. He was still growing and developing. If God had let her have the baby early when she wanted to, he may not have been healthy.

Sometimes we pray, "God, give me this promise *right now*. God, I'm uncomfortable. These people aren't treating me right. God, business is slow." What we can't see is that something is not ready. Maybe it's another person who is going to be involved. God is still working on them. Maybe it's another situation that's going to be a part of your destiny. It's not in place yet. Or maybe God is doing a work in you, developing your character, growing you stronger in that process. Whatever it is, it's in your best interest to wait on His perfect timing.

We read in Scripture that God didn't take the children of Israel the shortest route to the Promised Land because He knew they were not prepared for war (see Exodus 13:17). They thought they were ready. They had received God's promise of a land flowing with milk and honey. He had called them out of slavery, and they were on their way. But God basically said, "Not yet." God could see the big picture. He knew if He took them the shortest way, their enemies would be too powerful, and they would be defeated. So, *on purpose*, God took them a longer route to protect them and to strengthen them so that they could fulfill their destiny.

If something is not happening on your timetable, remind yourself, "God knows what He is doing. He has my best interests at heart. I wouldn't be having this delay unless God had a very good reason for it." And while you're waiting, don't make the mistake of trying to figure everything out. "God, I've been praying for my child for three years. Why won't he change? Did I do something wrong? Do I lack the faith? Is this a generational curse? Who in our family needs to repent? What if I tried this or that? What other resources can I find to help?" If you're constantly trying to figure things out, that's only going to frustrate you. Turn it over to God, and with faith and patience, trust His perfect timing. The thing He promised you, the thing you are praying for is on its way. When the time is right, you will receive what's yours.

Declaration

God, my times are in Your hands. I'm not going to worry about why something hasn't happened yet. I'm not going to worry about why it's taking so long. God, I trust You. I know at the set times, everything You promised me will come to pass. I will wait with faith and patience for Your perfect timing.

Wait for
Your Isaac

The biggest mistake we can make when we get in a hurry to see our prayers answered is to try to take matters into our own hands. We try to force things to happen rather than waiting on God's perfect timing. As a result, many times we miss God's best.

This is what happened with Abraham and Sarah. God gave them the promise that they were going to have a baby. But year after year went by, decade after decade, and nothing was happening. Abraham and Sarah are recorded in the hall of fame of faith (see Hebrews 11), but there is no mention of them in the hall of fame of patience. Instead of waiting for the begotten son, they decided to try to help God out. Sarah came up with a plan. She told Abraham to sleep with one of her maids, and they could raise that baby as their baby. Instead of waiting for God's timing, instead of trusting the promise, Abraham went along with the plan. Sure enough, they had a baby boy. They were jubilant over the child and named him Ishmael. They said, "Look! This is the child God promised us."

But God said, "Abraham, Sarah. That is not the child I promised you. That's something that you did on your own."

Do you know Ishmael was a struggle to raise? They were constantly having problems with him. Conflict surrounded him. There was no grace for him. What God gives birth to, God will always give you the grace to take care of. But when we birth things in our own strength, out of God's timing, then God is not obligated to make it easy for us.

Fourteen years later, at the set time, Sarah gave birth to Isaac, the child that God promised them. Like Sarah, there will be times in life where something is not happening as fast as you would like. You'll be tempted to try to force things to happen, to take matters into your own hands. Maybe you are in a relationship with someone who you know down deep isn't good for you. They don't treat you with respect, but you're afraid that you might not meet anyone else. No, if you'll let go of Ishmael, Isaac will show up. "The one" God promised you is in your future. The time has already been set. Now be patient, and trust God to do it His way.

Keep honoring God with your life, stay in peace, trust His timing, and He will open doors that no man can shut.

I learned a long time ago God doesn't need our help. He's got it all figured out. He knows the end from the beginning. All you have to do is trust Him. You don't have to try to force doors to open. You don't have to try to make people like you. Just keep honoring God with your life, stay in peace, trust His timing, and He will open doors that no man can shut. God will bring amazing people across your path. God will defeat your enemies and get you to where you're supposed to be.

Don't go around birthing Ishmaels when God wants to give you an Isaac. That's what it means in the Psalms when it says: "*Delight yourself also in the LORD, and He shall **give you** the desires of your heart*" (Psalm 37:4, NKJV, emphasis mine). There's a big difference between God giving you something and you having to work to make it happen. When we try to force things, we don't wait for God's timing. It's a constant struggle. It's a burden.

We can't seem to ever get it off the ground. But if you'll let God do it His way, in His timing, there'll be a supernatural grace. There will be an ease. Yes, you'll have opposition, but you'll feel a strength, a peace, and God's favor supernaturally pushing you forward. In other words, if you will wait for the set time, if you will be patient and not give birth to Ishmaels, then God has an Isaac in your future.

Now do your part and rest. Stay in peace. Trust God's timing. God knows what He is doing. We may not always understand why something is taking so long, but sometimes God will delay an answer on purpose simply so He can show his power in a greater way. He has something better for you. Wait for your Isaac.

Declaration

God, I want Your best for my life. Help me wait for the Isaac You have for me. In Jesus' name, Amen.

God Will
Fight for You

When Moses led the Israelites out of Egypt and out
of slavery, they thought their problems were over.
Pharaoh had let the people go. They no longer had
to make bricks, day in and day out. God had given
them favor with the Egyptians, and they went out
rich. They were on their way, a three-days' journey,
to the Promised Land.

As soon as he let them go, however, Pharaoh had
a change of heart. His heart was hardened against
the Israelites once again, and he wanted his slaves
back. He gathered his army, including 600 chariots,
and they pursued the Hebrew children.

The Israelites were terrified. "Why didn't you just let us die in Egypt?" they complained to Moses. They were surrounded by a huge army; greatly outnumbered. They were so worried, so stressed out. They were trying to come up with some type of strategy to fight off the enemy when Moses told them to relax. Chill out. There is nothing to worry about: "*Don't be afraid. Just stand still and watch the LORD rescue you today. The Egyptians you see today will never be seen again. The Lord himself will fight for you. Just stay calm.*" (Exodus 14:13–14, NLT).

Don't be afraid. Stand still. Stay calm, and the Lord will fight for you.

Notice who is in charge here. *God* will turn it around. *God* will restore you. *God* will vindicate you if you will be still and remain at rest.

Some of you today are facing a big challenge. You can't sleep well at night. You're upset. You're frustrated. God is saying to you what He said to them, "Be still. I've got it all figured out. I control the whole universe. I've already set the time to deliver you. I've already set the time to not only bring you out but to bring you out better off than you were before. Relax. Don't be afraid. Stand still. Stay calm, and I will fight for you."

What happened next is one of the most well-known scenes in the Old Testament. After a good night's rest, Moses lifted his staff and God parted the waters. Scripture says that *"the people of Israel walked through the middle of the sea on dry ground, with walls of water on each side!"* (Exodus 14:22, NLT). They walked. They weren't running for their lives. They weren't in chaos. They walked, calmly and peacefully, trusting God to take care of the army behind them.

And take care He did. The Egyptians gave chase. They pursued the children of Israel. They were in a frenzy to reach them. It was chaos and confusion. They didn't even notice the walls of water on either side of them until those waters came crashing down on top of them, drowning every last one of them, while the Israelites stood safely on the other side.

The way to know that you are truly trusting God and His timing is that you will be at peace. You will be at rest. You won't be overwhelmed in your mind or scattered in your life. You won't be constantly fretting and worrying about how it will all play out or when, because you know that the Lord will fight for you. You know that He will not let the enemy overtake you. You know that your job is faith, and His job is the fight. You'll be able to stand still and see the goodness of the Lord.

What battle are you facing that God wants to fight for you? Is it a fight for your marriage? A fight for a promotion? A fight for your health and your life? God is asking you to stand still. He is asking you to stay in faith. He is asking you to trust His timing. "Keep calm and carry on," He is saying, "because I will fight for you!"

Declaration

God, I choose to stay in peace. Even when there is a wall in front of me and an army behind me, I choose to stand still, to keep calm, and to focus on how big You are, not how big my problems are. No matter what enemies I face, I believe that You are on my side. I know that You will fight for me, I need only be still.

Be Still
and Know

A couple of years after my father died, I really wanted to write a book. I had a strong desire, but I didn't know any publishers or anything about the book industry. Several times I started to call a friend that did know a publisher, but I didn't feel good about it. I just knew it wasn't right. Over the next couple of years, I was approached by different publishers and even offered a contract. On the surface it looked good. They were fine people but down in my spirit, I could hear a still, small voice telling me, "Joel, be patient. This is not the right one. Trust My timing. Something better is coming."

I put it on hold month after month. I didn't worry about it. I wasn't frustrated. My attitude was, "God, my times are in Your hands. When You want me to write a book, I know You will open up the doors."

Timing is everything. Even though writing the book was the right thing, if I had forced it at the wrong time, I would have missed God's best. We need to be patient and let God open doors for us. Yes, you may have to knock. You'll have to put forth the effort. The book won't write itself! I'm a believer in being aggressive and pursuing dreams, but you don't have to force doors to open. You don't have to try to make people to like you. You don't have to talk yourself into it. If you'll be patient and wait for God's timing, He will give you the desires of your heart.

One day through a series of unusual events I met a publisher. I knew they were the right people. I felt good about it. Everything fell into place. And that book, *Your Best Life Now*, went on to become a huge success, published in over 40 languages. It has been a number-one *New York Times* bestseller and has sold over eight million copies. That's what happens when you wait for God's timing!

So often we think we have to do it only in our own strength. This is when many people make quick decisions that end up only making matters worse. The Scripture says, "*Be still, and know that I am God*" (Psalm 46:10, NIV). When you feel over-whelmed, and you're tempted to take everything into your own hands, you have to make yourself be still. You have to remember who God is and who He is to you. The battle is not yours. The battle is the Lord's. But as long as you're fighting it, trying to make it happen your way, trying to pay somebody back, being upset and worried all the time, then God is going to step back and let you do it on your own. But when you take it out of your hands and say, "God, I trust You. I know You have already set the time to bring me out. You've already set the time to vindicate me. You've set the time to bring healing. You've set the time to elevate me to the bestsellers list. I'm going to be still and know that You are God."

It may not happen overnight, but it will happen because He is God, and He has a good plan for your life.

This principle is especially important when we're facing challenges. It's easy to get all wrought up and think, "I need to make this happen NOW." No, you don't. If God isn't making it happen for you, then it's not your time yet. Wait on Him. Trust His timing. Trust the connections He will bring to you. When you wait on Him, He can take you from wanna-be writer to *New York Times* bestselling author. He can take you from the band room to platinum recording artist. He can take you from single to married with children. He can take you from uneducated to graduating with a master's degree. He can take you from sick to whole. It may not happen overnight, but it will happen because He is God, and He has a good plan for your life.

Declaration

God, I know who You are. You are CEO of my life. I am done trying to make things happen on my own. I don't want to live worried and stressed out anymore. I trust You with my life. I trust You for breakthrough. My times are in Your hands.

Whose Report Are You Going to Believe?

God said in Isaiah 60:22, "*At the right time, I, the LORD, will make it happen*" (NLT). When God put the promise in your heart, when He gave you that dream, He determined the right time to bring it to pass. He's already scheduled your healing, your breakthrough, your promotion. The news report doesn't matter. The medical report doesn't matter. The job market doesn't matter. The economy doesn't matter. There are right time moments in your future where things will fall into place, the right people will show up, and opportunity will find you. What you're believing for may not have happened yet, but when you understand that God has a right time, that it's already been scheduled by the Creator of the universe, you won't live worried, frustrated, wondering, "Is it ever going to happen?" You'll stay in peace, knowing that your right time is coming.

I talked to a man who was diagnosed with cancer of the kidney. They were able to remove the kidney, but when they tested his lymph nodes, the test came back positive. The cancer had spread all through his body. The doctors gave him less than two years to live.

That was one report, but God has another report. Sometimes medical science comes to the end of what they can do. They run out of options. There was no more treatment they could give him. In Isaiah 53, the prophet asks, *Whose report are you going to believe?* (v. 1). I'm not saying to deny your problems or act like they don't exist, but you do have to choose to believe what God says about you and not what people say about you.

People can talk you out of your miracle if you listen to their report instead of God's. This man was very respectful, but he told his doctors that he didn't believe he was finished, that he had more to do, and he was going to defy the odds. His primary doctor said, "Sir, you're in denial. You need to accept it and deal with it." Instead, the man came to the cancer hospital in Houston to get a second opinion. On the way, he stopped by our worship service and asked us to pray. I told him the same thing I would tell you: God has the final say. He can do what medicine cannot do. When you believe all things are possible, the right time for your miracle is coming.

The experts at the cancer hospital studied all of the man's records that were sent over from the first hospital, and they agreed with the initial diagnosis. They said, "It looks like they're correct; the cancer has spread all over." The man asked if they would take new tests. They didn't see any need for it. It hadn't been that long, but they went ahead and ran all new tests. A week later the cancer specialist sat the man down and said, "In all my years of practicing, I've never seen this. We can't find any cancer in your body." The initial scan showed cancer everywhere, but by the second scan, it was completely gone.

When it's your right time and what experts say is impossible, God says, "I, the Lord, will make it happen." God is asking you, "Is there anything too hard for the Lord?" You don't know what God is up to. There are supernatural results in your future. It's the hand of God that defies the odds, that thrusts you into places you can't go on your own, that makes a way where there was no way. When you come into your right time, all the forces of darkness cannot stop what God has planned. At the right time, your healing will come; at the right time, the person of your dreams will show up; at the right time, your business will take off. At the right time, you will come out of that addiction, that depression, that trouble at work, and live in freedom, wholeness, and victory. Don't get discouraged because it hasn't happened yet; your right time is coming. What you're up against may look bigger, stronger, and more powerful than you, but it's no match for our God. Stay in peace. You have the most powerful force in the universe on your side.

Declaration

God, I declare that there is nothing too hard for You. Where there is no way, there is Yahweh. You are more powerful than any troubles that can come against me. I will stay in peace because my trust is in You, my Lord and my God.

Therefore, I tell you, whatever you ask for in prayer, believe that you have received it, and it will be yours.

Mark 11:24, NIV

A Greater
Miracle

Making up
for Lost Time

We've all been through seasons in life where it feels like we've lost time. We were in a relationship that didn't work out; we've lost those years. We weren't raised in a healthy environment; it feels like we lost our childhood. We came down with an illness or struggled with an addiction; months passed, maybe years. We see it as time that we can't get back.

That's true in the natural, but we serve a supernatural God. He knows how to make up for lost time. He's not just going to restore you; He's going to restore the years that you spent in a relationship that didn't make it. That company that you've spent years at, and they haven't treated you fairly — God is not just going to turn it around, but He's going to pay you back for what should have been yours. He's not going to just bring you out of that illness; He's going to restore the years that you spent taking the treatment.

He saw you working hard, raising those children, and making sacrifices, but they haven't turned out like they should have. He saw you taking the treatment, keeping a good attitude, praising Him when it wasn't improving, and thanking Him when you didn't feel well. He saw you struggling with that addiction, trying to beat it, going to counseling, and quoting the promises even when you didn't see change. He saw you, and He is going to restore to you what you lost — what is rightfully yours.

But here's how good God is: He is even going to restore the years that we wasted, making poor choices and running with the wrong crowd. He is going to restore the years you should have been studying but spent partying instead. He is going to restore the years that you should have been raising your children, but you were distracted doing other things. He is going to restore the years you should have been pursuing your dreams, but you let fear and opposition hold you back.

It should be too late. You think you missed your chance. But God is saying, "Get ready. I'm about to restore the years." He is going to make up for that time you missed pursuing your calling. He is going to make up for that time you spent sick and in the hospital. He is going to make up for the time you wasted on the wrong relationship, the wrong job, the wrong crowd. He is going to make up for the time you missed with your children. He is not going to just restore the relationship you have with them; He's going to restore the years. He's going to make it as if you never lost that time.

In retrospect, some things feel like they were a waste of time, but God is going to make the rest of your life so fulfilling that you don't think about what you went through.

Job was a man after God's own heart. He was faithful to God, faithful on behalf of his children, and loyal to his friends. God blessed him with a wife and children, with work that he enjoyed, and with a number of friends and colleagues. The enemy thought that Job's loyalty to God was based on what God gave him, so he convinced God to let him snatch it all away. Job lost everything. He lost his wealth, his family, his friends, his employees, his livestock, his fields, and his health. But God didn't forget about Job; and God not only restored to him what he had lost, but He blessed him more in his future than he had in his past. The Bible says in Job 42:12, "*Now the LORD blessed the latter days of Job more than his beginning"* (NKJV). Job was given twice as many animals as he had before. He was given more children to raise, more employees to lead, and I'll bet even his wife was nicer to live with.

Your latter days will be better than your former days too. God wants to make up for lost time. He wants to give you everything you've ever wanted and more, all to His glory.

Declaration

God, we can't go back in time in the natural, but You are a supernatural God; and I believe that You can make up for lost time and restore to me every second that I lost, wasted, or missed. My future is in Your hands!

He Restores the Years

God said in Joel 2:25, *"And I will restore to you the years that the locust hath eaten, the cankerworm, and the caterpiller, and the palmerworm, My great army which I sent among you"* (KJV).

In this passage, the Israelites had planted their crops, watered them, and did their best to keep the weeds out. Everything was going great, and the crops took off. But when they were about to harvest them, swarms of locusts came in like a mighty army and ate all of the crops.

I'm sure the Israelites were discouraged. It wasn't fair. They had worked hard but had nothing to show for it. They made it through that winter, however, even holding to their faith, still believing that God was in control. The next year they went out and planted their crops again. They thought, "That setback can't stop us. We didn't have a harvest last year, but God sustained us. We'll have one this year." But when the crops were ready to harvest, here came the locusts, just like the year before. When they saw them over the horizon, I can imagine how their hearts sank. As they sat there and watched millions of locusts slowly eat up their crops, it was like pouring salt on a wound.

This didn't happen just in one year. This didn't just happen in two years. But for four consecutive years, their harvest was completely wiped out. Four consecutive years!

The Israelites were tempted to think, "There's no use even planting. It's not worth the effort. We know what's going to happen. These locusts are going to be right back."

Maybe you are believing for your health to improve, but every time you go for a checkup, it's the same negative report. Maybe you are being your best at work, but you never get promoted. Like with the Israelites, it feels like your harvest is being eaten. You're doing the right thing, but the locusts keep showing up.

While the Israelites were discouraged, thinking they would never see a harvest, God spoke to them through the prophet Joel. He said in effect, "I know it hasn't been fair. I've seen what didn't work out. I've seen what's been stolen. I'm not going to just stop the locusts; I'm not going to just give you a harvest this season; I'm going to restore the years that were stolen. I'm going to give you this season's harvest, plus four more harvest seasons." That's how good God is. He's going to make up for the years that you've lost. This wasn't just a promise for the Israelites. It is a promise for you too.

The Scripture says, *"The threshing floors shall be full of wheat, and the vats shall overflow with new wine and oil. . . . You shall eat in plenty and be satisfied, And praise the name of the Lord your God, who has dealt wondrously with you; and My people shall never be put to shame"* (Joel 2:24, 26, NKJV).

Notice what happens when God restores: abundance, overflow, and more than enough. The Israelites had been in famine, struggling, not seeing any increase; and suddenly, God not only turned it around, but He paid them back for the lost years. He restored the years that the locusts had eaten. He made up for what should have been theirs.

God is keeping a record of everything that should have been yours. He knows what you didn't get, and He knows that you have been faithful while you waited for your set time. Your harvest hasn't come yet, but don't worry, it's on the way.

God is not going to just free you, just heal you, just turn your children around. He's going to restore the years that you've lost. You're going to get the harvest from all those years you prayed, all those years you believed, all those years you did the right thing. That harvest has been stored up. The enemy may think he took it, but God has the final say. He has blessings stored up for you. When He restores the years, you're going to be more fulfilled than you've ever been.

Declaration
God, I trust You to restore the years that I have lost. When my harvest comes, my life will overflow with blessings, overflow with joy, and overflow with favor because You don't just bless; You bless with abundance.

Stored-up Blessings

A man I know was married at a young age. They struggled as a young couple and had some rough years, but he was determined to make it work. He worked overtime to love and forgive and go the extra mile. They had two children, but at one point, the wife checked out. She was done. This man kept being his best, raising the children basically by himself. The wife was still there, but she wouldn't have much to do with him. He kept praying, believing, and asking God to turn it around; but on his 25th wedding anniversary, she left a note saying she was leaving.

This man was so heartbroken. When I saw him, he looked like he had aged 20 years. He was normally so upbeat, fun, and positive; but it was like all the life had been drained out of him. I tried to encourage him and let him know that there were still good days ahead, but he was so down. He said, "I've invested all this time — I've poured out my heart and soul trying to make my marriage work, and it was all for nothing."

It wasn't for nothing. God sees the years you've lost. He knows the pain, the hurt, and what wasn't fair. The beauty of our God is He doesn't just heal the wounds; He restores the years. He'll make up for what wasn't fair.

You may feel like you're in one of those lost years now. Business is slow. You've put your dreams on hold. You're dealing with an illness. Your child is off course. You've invested so much, but it looks like it was time and money and energy wasted. Stay encouraged! Payback is coming.

God is keeping the records. He knows how to not just restore you but restore the years that were stolen. The years that were unfair, the years that were lonely, the years you struggled with that depression, that anxiety, that addiction. When God restores the years, you're not going to look like what you've been through. When He makes up for what should have been yours, nobody is going to know that you had that illness; nobody will know that you went through that breakup; nobody will know that you ever struggled as a parent. You'll be so blessed, so happy, and so healthy that nobody will be able to tell.

Over time, my friend began to get his passion back, his faith back, and his vision back. Instead of living defeated, he started thanking God that there was beauty for those ashes, that what was meant for harm God was turning to his advantage. Three years later, he met a beautiful young lady. They fell in love and ended up getting married. I'll never forget what he told me. He said, "Joel, I have never been this happy in all my life. I never dreamed I could be this fulfilled. I didn't know what a healthy relationship was." What was that? God restoring the years that were lost. God knows how to make up for what should have been yours. Just because it hasn't happened doesn't mean that it's not going to happen. God is storing up what belongs to you.

I believe He's about to release some of those stored-up blessings. When He restores the years, you'll see increase that you've never seen, blessings that catapult you ahead, and divine connections with people who are better for you than you've ever imagined. You, no doubt, feel like you've lost some time, some years; but the good news is it's only temporary. Everything that belongs to you is coming back. The health, the freedom, the promotion, the joy, and the victory — it's all coming back. It's not coming back like it was; it's going to be pressed down, shaken together, and running over with goodness. When God restores the years, like with my friend, it will be better and healthier and more fulfilling than you ever thought to imagine.

Declaration

God, thank You for my stored-up blessings. I am about to come into my season of abundance — abundant health, abundant resources, and abundant opportunities. I may be in one of those lost years now, but I am determined to be faithful. It's not for nothing. Favor is on its way!

Rightfully Yours

The Israelites were stuck in slavery for many years. They were mistreated, forced to work long hours, and given quotas that were impossible to meet. Despite how unfair it was, they kept working hard and being their best, but not seeing any increase. They thought it was permanent; they had already accepted that they would never be free. But God sees when you're doing the right thing and still being mistreated. He sees when you're not reaping any harvest.

It may feel like God has forgotten about you. You've accepted that you'll always struggle, always be at a disadvantage, and always have that trouble at work. But that's not the case! Your time is coming. God said in Exodus 3:7–8,

> *I have surely seen the oppression of My people who are in Egypt, and have heard their cry because of their taskmasters, for I know their sorrows. So I have come down to deliver them out of the hand of the Egyptians, and to bring them up from that land to a good and large land, to a land flowing with milk and honey.* (NKJV)

I have seen the affliction of My people. I have heard their cry. I am coming down to deliver them. God was saying in effect, "Enough is enough." There will be a time when God says, "That's it. I'm coming down to vindicate you, to heal you, to free you, to promote you, and to pay you back for what you're owed."

The Pharaoh that was holding them captive was very powerful. He had a huge army, the latest equipment, all these chariots, and skilled warriors. The Israelites had none of that. They had no chance against him in the natural. They were slaves. They owned nothing. But God is not limited by what you don't have, by who is against you, by how powerful the sickness looks, by how long you've struggled with the addiction, or by how far that child is off course. Nothing can stand against our God. When He comes down to deliver you, all the forces of darkness cannot stop Him.

Don't focus on how big your obstacles are; focus on how big your God is. He spoke worlds into existence; He flung stars into space. He is saying to you what He said to them, "I see you. I hear you. I'm on my way. I'm coming down to deliver you. I'm coming down to make things happen that you couldn't make happen. I'm coming down to restore the years that you lost."

God sent plague after plague on the Pharaoh and his people. He was stubborn, but he finally agreed to let them go. I'm sure the Israelites were thrilled to be free. It was a day they never dreamed would happen. They were satisfied to just be leaving, but God wasn't satisfied. He doesn't just bring you out; He restores the years that were stolen. He pays you back for what should have been yours.

On their way out, God said, *"I will give this people favor in the sight of the Egyptians; and it shall be, when you go, that you shall not go empty-handed"* (Exodus 3:21, NKJV). God caused the Israelites to have favor with their oppressors, and they gave them their gold, their silver, and their clothing. One version says they left loaded down with blessings. Another version says they were *"leaving bondage with great possessions that are rightfully yours*" (v. 22, AMP). What was that? God paying them back for 430 years of working as slaves.

God is keeping the records of what you are owed — what is *"rightfully yours."* Those times you've done the right thing but got the wrong result. You did your best, but you didn't get promoted, the loan didn't go through, and the anxiety didn't go away. Despite it all, you kept believing, praising God, and being good to others. Like the Israelites, your time is coming. God is storing up the harvest that should have been yours. What God has for you is still on the way.

Declaration

God, I believe You when You say my time is coming, when I will be out of this bondage and I will take possession of what is rightfully mine — joy, success, healing, good relationships, victory, and a land flowing with milk and honey. My future is in Your hands!

Redeem the Time

Our daughter Alexandra was born a month and a half before my father went to be with the Lord. During that time, my father was on dialysis, and many times I would take him to the clinic. It was a very busy season. Then when he went to be with the Lord, our whole life changed. I was thrust into the pastor's role, and I was doing my best to just stay afloat. I don't remember very well the first couple of years of Alexandra's life. We were in such transition, and I was learning how to minister and trying to figure everything out. It consumed me.

Several years later I realized that I didn't have the same memories of Alexandra's first few years like

I did with our son Jonathan. I remember saying to God, almost in passing, "God, I'm asking you to restore the years and redeem the time that I lost with my daughter by being so busy and so preoccupied with other things."

Alexandra was eight years old when I prayed that prayer, and all she wanted to do was be with her dad. She would rather go out in the backyard and let me watch her do cartwheels than go over to a friend's house. We spent so much time together that sometimes I needed a break, so I would say, "Why don't you go swimming with your cousins, or why don't you have your friends over?" She'd say, "No, Dad, I want to stay here with you." We were the best of friends. All these years later and we're still the best of friends. You know what that is: God restoring the years and redeeming the time.

I was at a book signing years ago when I met a woman who was estranged from her daughter. They hadn't spoken to each other in years. The mother had reached out to her daughter many times but with no success. She was discouraged until she heard me talking about how God can redeem the time and give us another chance. Faith rose in her heart. She said, "God, do that for me." Months later she came to the book signing. Out of the hundreds of people there, she noticed that her daughter was in line. She hadn't seen her in person in years. She went over to her, and they embraced. While they wept, healing was taking place. When they came up to the table to have their books signed, they were both still weeping. The mother told me how she didn't know her daughter watched us on television. She had no idea she'd be at that book signing, but that was a divine appointment and the beginning of God redeeming the time they had lost.

God is not going to just redeem you; He's going to redeem the time. He's going to give you another chance.

God is going to do that for you. He's going to redeem opportunities that you missed. He's going to redeem relationships that are not what they should be. He's going to redeem the years that you lost not making good decisions, when you were giving in to compromise. You don't have to live in regret, thinking you missed your season, that it's too late to accomplish your dream, or too late to have good relationships with your family. There is not too much water under the bridge. God is not going to just redeem you; He's going to redeem the time. He's going to give you another chance. Don't believe those lies that you're too old or you've made too many mistakes. You wouldn't be reading this if God wasn't about to redeem the time.

You may have missed out on some things while you were distracted and focused on the wrong things. Don't worry. God can redeem the time. He's about to bring something across your path that should have been yours years ago. You missed it the first time, like I did with Alexandra, but God's about to give you another chance. He's about to redeem the time. It's not too late for you to have good relationships; it's not too late for you to accomplish your dreams. It's not too late.

Declaration

God, I believe that You can redeem the time. I lost some important years while I was distracted by many things. But now I am ready to focus on You and the things that You want for my life. Thank You for restoring the years and redeeming the time.

A Greater Miracle

In Mark 5, a leader in the synagogue came to Jesus. He fell at Jesus' feet and said, "Jesus, my little girl is very sick, she's close to death. Please come to my house and pray for her." Jesus agreed. They started heading that way. I can imagine how excited the man was. He knew his daughter was going to get her miracle. But as they were walking, surrounded by a huge crowd, a lady came up that had been sick for twelve years. She fought her way through the crowd and touched the hem of Jesus' robe. She was instantly healed. Jesus stopped and said, "Who touched me?" He spent time talking with the lady, explaining how her faith made her whole.

While it was a great miracle, it delayed Jesus from getting to the man's house where his little girl was sick. I'm sure this father was happy that the lady got healed, maybe even encouraged that, because Jesus healed the woman, He could heal the little girl too. But the delay ended up being costly. The man's friends came and met them on the road and said, "Don't bother Jesus. It's too late; your daughter has died."

This man had just watched somebody else get healed while his daughter didn't get healed. A much older woman was now healthy and whole while his little girl was dead.

Can you stay in faith when you see other people being blessed, but you're still waiting? Your friend got engaged, but you're still single. Your cousin moved into his new house, but you're still in a tiny apartment. Your coworker got a good medical report, but you're still taking the treatment. Your partner got a promotion, but you can't catch a break. Can you be happy when others get what you want? Can you keep your peace while you wait? Can you keep believing when the thing you are believing for has died?

In all the commotion, in all the excitement, this man felt like Jesus had forgotten about him. Now it was too late — he was ready to walk away. But Jesus said to him, "Don't be afraid; just believe."

What is impossible in the natural is possible with God.

He's saying the same thing to you: "It's not too late. I haven't forgotten about you. You're still right on schedule; your steps are ordered. This delay didn't stop My plan. I'm still going to do what I promised. What is impossible in the natural is possible with Me."

Jesus walked the rest of the way home with the man, to the house where the man's little girl had already died. Jesus said to the girl, "Wake up!" And she woke back up and was perfectly well. The Scripture says in Mark 5:42, *"they were completely astonished"* (NIV).

Here's the principle: this man came to Jesus asking for healing, but because of the delay, he received a greater miracle: a resurrection. When you have to wait a long time, don't get discouraged; that means God has something bigger planned for you, something better, something you weren't expecting. Like Jesus did for this man, He's going to do something where not only you, but the people around you are going to be astonished, amazed, and overwhelmed at the goodness of God.

Your situation may be taking longer than you thought. Maybe it's something more difficult than you've ever experienced. Everyone else is getting their miracle, but you are still waiting. That doesn't mean that the enemy is getting the best of you. It doesn't mean that God went on vacation and is not concerned anymore. No, God has not turned it around yet because He wants to show His favor in your life in an amazing way. God is going to show His strength, His healing, His goodness, and His power like you've never seen before. You might as well get ready. God has a greater miracle in mind for you. God is going to resurrect something in your life, and when He does, everybody around you is going to have no doubt the God you serve is an awesome God.

Declaration

God, I know that the reason I haven't experienced my breakthrough yet is because You have an even greater miracle for me in mind. I trust that my steps are ordered. I will not settle for anything less than Your best for me.

My Times Are in Your Hands

I have a digital clock on my bathroom counter at home. It gets its information from a satellite, like the clock on your cell phone. A while back, I was about to get in the shower one evening and noticed that it was 9:30 p.m. A few minutes later, when I got out of the shower, I looked at the clock, and it read 9:22 p.m. I thought, "That's strange; I know it was just 9:30!" I thought I must have read it wrong, but while I was watching it, the clock went back to 9:18. In a few seconds, it went to 9:07. It kept backing up in time!

I realized it must have been getting bad reception, but I had never seen that happen before. What's interesting is, that day I had a very busy schedule. I had a lot to do, but I hardly got anything done. I had interruptions, delays, and things that didn't work out. I was frustrated, thinking, "What an unproductive day!" But when I saw that clock go backwards, it was as if God was saying to me, "Joel, quit worrying about what you didn't get done. I control time. I can back things up. I can turn back time!"

God *can* turn back time. He can give you back the days, the hours, the years that you have missed. He can also propel you forward, moving you to the head of the line, promoting you before it is your turn, skipping over months and years that you should have had to go through to earn your new position.

David said in Psalm 31:15, *"My times are in Your hands"* (NIV). Whether God is opening doors that no man can shut or choosing to keep a door closed in front of you for a season, He is in control. He controls the universe, and He controls time.

When David wrote that psalm, he was in a tough season. He hadn't yet received the promotion, the vindication, the breakthrough, or the victory. But he chose to say, "My times are in Your hands. I trust You where I am. I am not discouraged. I am not frustrated. I am not stressed out. You will make things happen that I can't make happen. You will get me to my destiny, and I won't be one second late!"

God has not forgotten about you. He has seen everything you've been through, the hurts, the struggles, and the lonely nights. The Scripture says, *"You have collected all my tears"* (Psalm 56:8, NLT). He sees every tear, and He's not going to just bring you out of this tough season; He's going to bring you out better.

I spoke to a woman who was raised in a rough environment. Her mother and father weren't around. At fifteen, she was living on the streets. She got into drugs and other harmful things. She ended up in prison. She had such low self-esteem; she didn't feel any sense of value. It seemed unfair that she'd had all these bad breaks at such a young age with no one to give her guidance or watch after her. While in prison, however, she started watching us on television. She'd never had anyone speak faith into her and tell her who she was. She heard me talking about how we are children of the Most High God, how God has handpicked us and called us a masterpiece, how we have seeds of greatness, how no weapon formed against us will prosper. She gave her life to Christ right there in the prison. Her whole outlook changed. A few years later, she was released. Against all odds, today she owns her own business. She's happily married with children. She volunteers here at the church. She never dreamed that she would be this blessed — this fulfilled.

You may have been through some bad breaks, too, but that didn't stop your destiny. God knows how to get you to where you're supposed to be. Instead of thinking of all the reasons it's not going to happen, turn it around and say, "God, You control time, and my times are in Your hands!"

Declaration

God, thank You for fulfilling Your promises in my life, moving me into my destiny at the right time. You have the power to both turn back time and to propel me forward. My times are in Your hands!

The Big Picture

God can see the big picture for our lives. He knows
what's up ahead. He knows what we're going to need,
who we're going to need, and when they need to
show up. If God did everything we asked, on our
timetable, it would limit us, because sometimes
what we're asking for is too small. Sometimes the
person we think we can't live without, God knows
in 10 years they're not going to be good for us,
so He is closing the door right now. If right now,
God gave us that promotion we want so badly, He
knows it would keep us from a much bigger promotion that He has three years down the road. God
has the advantage of seeing it all. The longer I live,
the more I trust Him. So many times I have looked
back and said, "God, thank You for not answering
that prayer. God, thank You for not letting that person
into my life." God knows what He is doing.

God said, "When the time is right, I will make it happen." The beauty is, we don't have to make it happen. You don't have to manipulate things, force a door to open, or make yourself get well. God is going to make it happen. You may have obstacles that are too big for you. You don't see how you can get out of debt, how you can have a baby, or how you can accomplish a dream. The good news is you're not on your own. At the right time, God will open the doors, He will cause you to conceive, and He will turn your child around.

At the right time, I walked into a jewelry store to buy a watch battery and met the woman of my dreams. At the right time, a city council member changed their vote, and we acquired the Compaq Center. At the right time, God stepped in and healed my mother of terminal cancer. At the right time, David took a sling shot and defeated Goliath. At the right time, prison doors flung open for Paul and Silas. You may not see how this could happen; the odds are against you. You're looking at it in the natural, but our God is supernatural. He's not limited by what limits us. He sees the big picture and the right time moments in your future, where He's going to make things happen that you could never make happen.

Now here's the key: if there's a right time, that means any other time is the wrong time. God knows what He's doing. He can see the big picture.

If it hasn't happened yet, it hasn't been the right time. You have to trust Him. It doesn't mean it's not going to happen. God has not forgotten about you. Your right time is already on the schedule. If it would have happened sooner, it wouldn't have been a blessing. In the waiting process, God is doing a work in us, getting us stronger, developing our character, and preparing us to carry the weight of glory. If the situation is not changing, maybe God is using the situation to change you. If it's not working out yet, maybe He's working out something in you. The test is, will you trust Him while you're waiting for the right time? Will you keep a good attitude, will you stay in faith when you don't see anything happening?

This is when it's easy to get discouraged, to live stressed, to wonder when God is going to turn it around, when you are going to meet Mr. Right (instead of Mr. Right Now!), when your business is going to grow, when people are going to start recognizing your gifts and talents. Why don't you relax and come back to a place of peace. God sees what you're going through. He knows what you need. He knows your dreams and your goals because He's the one who put them in you. What He has purposed for your life will come to pass.

Remember: God can see the big picture. He knows not only when you're ready but when other people are ready. While you're waiting, it may seem like nothing is happening, but behind the scenes, God is working.

Declaration

God, You know what's best for me. You see the big picture. I refuse to live frustrated. I choose to trust You and Your timing!

Something Bigger

God gave Abraham and Sarah a promise that they would have a baby. If God would have given them this promise when they were in their twenties and thirties, when it was a normal time to have children, they would have believed it. But sometimes God will wait on purpose. He will wait until the odds are against us — when it seems like it's too late, we're too old, we don't have the training, the medical report is not good, and we don't come from an influential family. We have plenty of excuses to not believe. But when God gives the promise, He sets the time to bring it to pass. It's as good as done.

Like Abraham and Sarah — who were in their seventies and eighties when God promised them they would have a baby — what God has spoken to you may seem impossible, like it could never happen. Don't get talked out of your dream. Don't let doubt keep you from believing for what God promised. Thank God in advance that it's on the way.

What's interesting is that Sarah wanted a baby, but God wanted a nation. Sarah would have been thrilled to give birth to a son, but God was setting up something much bigger. God said in Genesis 17:16, *"I will bless her and will surely give you a son by her. I will bless her so that she will be the mother of nations; kings of peoples will come from her"* (NIV). She not only had a son at ninety years old, but she gave birth to nations; kings came out of her.

Your right times are coming and they're going to be better than you thought.

Maybe the reason your dream is taking longer, the reason that promise hasn't come to pass yet is because what God is going to do is going to be so much bigger, so much more fulfilling than what you have in mind. You're not going to give birth to a son, but to a nation. You're not going to give birth to a peasant, but to a king. When you see how God shows out in your life, you're going to be amazed.

The Scripture says Sarah laughed when she had that son. She even named him Isaac, which means laughter. The first time, when she heard the promise, she laughed in unbelief, thinking, "There's no way." This time, when she saw the promise, she laughed in amazement, thinking, "Wow, God, I never dreamed this could happen." I love how merciful God is. He could have said, "Fine, Sarah. If you think it's impossible; if you think it will never happen, then I'll find someone else." But God doesn't hold our lack of faith, our doubt, or our unbelief against us. You may have laughed in unbelief, thinking you could never get well, never get out of debt, never break that addiction, but I believe the second laugh is coming. You're going to laugh in amazement, overjoyed and full of wonder, thinking, "Wow, God, You've shown out in my life. Wow, God, You've done amazing things."

God has already scheduled wow moments for your life. He has scheduled things you never dreamed would happen — favor like you've never seen, new levels for your family, opportunities, healing, the right people, and abundance. Your right times are coming, and they're going to be better than you thought.

He puts it on the calendar, but how we wait is up to us. We can wait discouraged, "When is it going to happen? I thought You said I was going to meet someone, but it's been so long. I thought You said I was going to be a leader, but the dog won't even listen to me." Switch over into faith. Be a believer and not a doubter. "God, You said You'd make me the happy mother of children. I haven't been able to conceive yet, but I thank You that the right time is coming; there's a baby in my future." When you understand that God is going to make it happen, it takes the pressure off. You can relax. You can live in peace. You just keep honoring God, and He'll take you places that you've never dreamed. Trust that He's got something bigger planned for you!

Declaration

God, I know that sometimes You like to wait on purpose so that You can show out in my life. Even when the odds are against me in the natural, I trust that the promises You gave me will come to pass at the right time; and when they do, they will be bigger than I could ever imagine!

Closer Than
You Think

Jesus was at a wedding in Galilee. At one point during the festivities, they ran out of wine. This was a major catastrophe — a social taboo in this day and age. So Jesus' mother, Mary, came to Him and told Him about the problem. She said, *"They have no more wine."* Jesus responded, " *... that's not our problem ... My time has not yet come"* (John 2:3–4, NLT).

Up until then, Jesus had never performed a miracle. He had never healed a person, never walked on water, and never multiplied food, yet his mother could sense that He was close to stepping into a new level of His destiny. Deep down, she knew

He was going to impact the world; she just didn't know when.

When Jesus told her it wasn't the right time yet, Mary heard it; she understood what He was saying, but in faith, she told the assistants, "*Do whatever He tells you*" (v. 5). She was saying, "His time may not have come yet, but it's close. There's about to be a shift. He's on the verge of His right time — where He steps into His ministry, where a new level of favor, power, and miracles are released."

Just a few minutes after He said, "*My time has not yet come,*" He told the assistants to go fill the empty pots with water. As they were bringing them back, the water suddenly turned into wine. He went from "My time has not yet come" to "the right time is here" in a matter of moments. That was His first miracle. From then on, He went out and impacted the world.

When you look at your circumstances, the obstacles you're up against, how long you've been trying to accomplish your goals, you could say like Jesus, "My time has not yet come. I can't do anything about this challenge." But, like Mary could sense something new was about to happen with Jesus, I can sense that God is about to do something greater in your life. You wouldn't be reading this if you weren't about to come out of "my time has not yet come" into "my right time is here." You're on the verge of stepping into a new season — a season of greater favor, promotion, and healing. Things that have held you back in the past — barriers that have limited your family — those powers are being broken. You're going to see influence, resources, and talent coming out in ways you never dreamed. Problems that look permanent are about to suddenly turn around. Family members who wouldn't have anything to do with you, that strife and division are coming to an end. You don't have to make this happen. It's going to be the hand of God. You came into your right time.

He is about to do something greater in you and through you.

Like Mary said to those assistants, the key is: do whatever God asks you to do. If He asks you to wait, then wait. If He asks you to move, move. If He asks you to fill the water jugs, fill the water jugs. Keep being faithful even though you don't see anything happening. Keep believing for your healing, keep declaring you are blessed, keep thanking God that it will be a bountiful year. Your time may not have come yet, but it's closer than you think. There's about to be a shift: from struggling to ease, from barely making it to abundance, from fighting that addiction to freedom, from dealing with that sickness to health and wholeness, from closed doors and nothing working out to things falling into place. If you'll trust His timing and stay in faith, I believe and declare, you're about to come in to one of your "right-time" moments. Your water is about to become wine. The impossible is about to become possible. He is about to do something greater in you and through you. Healing, promotion, divine connections — they are all closer than you think.

Declaration

God, I declare that my time is coming, and it's closer than I think. A shift is coming. A new level is coming. I am about to step into my destiny. I trust You to make a way where there is no way and to take me to the next level of the future You have for me. In Jesus' name, Amen.

My times are in Your hands . . .

Psalm 31:15, NIV

Your Future Is in God's Hands

Out with the Old, in with the New

It's easy to get stuck in life. When we've gone through disappointments, had setbacks, tried and our dream didn't work out, we can settle where we are and think this is as good as it gets. But God said in Isaiah, "*See, I am doing a new thing! Now it springs up; do you not perceive it?*" (Isaiah 43:19, NIV). God is about to do something new in your life. He didn't create you to get stuck at one level and stay there. He has new opportunities, new relationships, and new favor.

It may look like you'll always struggle in your finances, but get ready, something new is coming. Promotion, opportunity, and open doors that you never dreamed would open. The medical report says you have to live with that sickness. God is saying, "I'm doing a new thing. I'm restoring health. I'm breathing energy, vitality, and freshness into your body." That child has been off course for years. You've accepted that he'll never change. That would be true, but God is doing a new thing. Forces of darkness are being broken. Purpose and destiny are rising up. You're about to see a turnaround. Maybe that addiction has hindered you your whole life. You've tried to stop, gone to counseling, but nothing helped. This is a new day. Chains that have held you back are being loosed. What's kept you in captivity is coming to an end. Now you have to do your part and receive the prophecy. You can't go around thinking you're stuck, the problem is too big, or that's it's been this way too long. Turn it around. "Lord, I believe what You promised; thank You that You're doing some new thing in my life."

When Isaiah prophesied this "new thing," the Israelites were in captivity in Babylon. They had been there a long time. Year after year, nothing changed for them. I'm sure they thought, "We'll always struggle; we'll always be oppressed." Then Isaiah showed up and said, "Get ready. God is doing a new thing." They could have thought, "Yeah right, have you seen these enemies? Look how powerful they are. All the circumstances say we're stuck — we'll never live an abundant life, we'll never own our own homes, our children will never be free." Don't talk yourself out of the new thing God wants to do. The odds may be against you, but the Most High God is for you.

The Israelites had been through many struggles. They had unfair things happen. They also made mistakes and brought trouble on themselves. They could have been sitting in self-pity, feeling hopeless and discouraged. But Isaiah said, "*Forget the former things; do not dwell on the past*" (v. 18, NIV). **Behold, God is doing a new thing!**

The principle is, if you're dwelling on the past, you won't see the new thing. If you're focused on who hurt you and what wasn't fair, then you'll miss your destiny. Living in regrets will keep you from new opportunities; reliving your mistakes will stop the new favor. As long as you're looking back at the old, you won't see the new.

Is there something you need to forget so you can see the new thing? Is there something you need to quit dwelling on so you can step into the favor and abundance that God has for you?

When someone hurts you, if you keep thinking about it, then you're letting them continue to hurt you. Don't give them your power. You have to let it go. Give it to God. He saw what they did. God sees your tears and your heartache. He has beauty for those ashes. But here's the key: you have to let go of the ashes before you can see the beauty. It's an exchange. God says, "You give me the ashes, you quit dwelling on the hurts, you forgive them, you move forward with your life, and I'll give you the beauty. I'll do something so great, so rewarding, that you won't even think about what you lost." The new thing God has for you, the new people, the new opportunities, the promotion, the healing, the influence will be better than you ever dreamed.

Declaration

God, You are ready to do a new thing in my life. I am letting go of the past to make room for the future. I believe that the new thing You have for me will be so great that I won't even miss the old!

Rivers in
the Desert

While the Israelites were in captivity, they were surrounded by desert wastelands. Even if they could have escaped their captors, they wouldn't have survived. But Isaiah prophesied that God would provide water in the wilderness and rivers in the desert (see Isaiah 43:20). What looked barren, He was about to turn into fertile land. He was going to do a new thing, but it wasn't going to be natural; it was going to be supernatural.

You cannot predict what God will do in your life because He defies logic. What God is about to do is going to be unusual, uncommon, and out of the ordinary. You're going to see rivers where there should be dry places. The Scripture says, "... *even in famine they will have more than enough*" (Psalm 37:19, NLT). It seems like in famine you would barely get by, but God does things that defy the odds. He makes rivers in the desert. He parts seas, cures lepers, and multiplies food to feed thousands.

A woman told me about receiving a small inheritance from a relative who had passed away. She decided to invest it in real estate. She bought a house and rented it out. Unfortunately, the people she rented it to turned out to be dishonest. Three months into the lease, they stopped paying rent. Eventually the house went into foreclosure. The woman could have been bitter and upset. She could have sued them and tried to get revenge. But, she said, "I didn't make a big deal about it."

Year after year, she kept being her best. Nobody even knew she went through the bad break because she was always so positive. She never complained. She was never discouraged. She kept moving forward with her life.

Six years later, she unexpectedly received a check in the mail from the bank. It was for $125,000. The enclosed letter said, "The property sold; this belongs to you." She hadn't even paid that much for the property in the first place! What looked like a bad break turned into a profit. What looked like a wasteland,

God turned into fertile ground. What seemed like a loss turned into a gain. What felt like a setback was really a setup for God to show out in her life.

The desert represents barrenness and no growth. It is when you are doing the right thing, but your business is not increasing, your marriage is not getting better, your health is not improving, and you were passed over for another promotion. In those dry places, you could be discouraged, thinking it will never change. Or you can get ready, knowing that God is about to make rivers in that desert. He's about to turn that barren land into fertile ground. Like what happened for this woman, you're going to see increase that you can't explain, favor that you didn't deserve, healing that doesn't make sense, and freedom from things that have held you back.

You have to be careful with your thoughts and your words because you can actually stop the prophecy from coming to pass. The psalmist said they "*limited the Holy One of Israel*" (Psalm 78:41, KJV). You can limit what God wants to do in your life by focusing on doubt, negativity, and speaking defeat. You are canceling out the prophecy when you repeatedly say, "My business is never going to grow. I'll never meet the right person. I will always be in debt. I just have to live with this sickness. Have you seen all that I've been through?"

You may have obstacles that look too big; you don't see how you can accomplish that dream. It feels like you're stuck, you're in captivity, you are restricted by your environment. God is saying to you what He said to the Israelites, "I'm making rivers in those deserts. I'm turning the barren places into fertile ground."

Start expecting God's favor; start believing for the unusual.

You may be in a dry place, but you're not going to stay there. Water is coming, favor is coming; promotion, healing, and freedom are coming. Get your hopes up. Start expecting God's favor; start believing for the unusual. Get in agreement with God, and receive all that He has for you.

Declaration

God, this is for me today. I receive it into my spirit. I'm getting ready for something unusual — something supernatural. Lord, amaze me with Your goodness. Turn this problem around. God show out in my life!

Present Tense

When God says He is doing a new thing (Isaiah 43:19), it is significant that this promise is in the present tense. He didn't say, *"I'm about to do a new thing. One day* I'm going to work in your life. *Sometime in the future* I'm going to show you My goodness."* God said, "I am doing a new thing." It's already started. What God has for you is already set in motion. This new thing is already in process.

The Scripture says, *"Now it springs forth ..."* (v. 19, AMPC). "Spring forth" is a phrase that describes when a seed is planted in the ground. You can't see anything happening, but the seed has opened up. It's springing forth even though it may not become visible for some time. There are promotions, healings, breakthroughs, and divine connections that have already sprung forth in your life. They're already en route. Just because you don't see them doesn't mean they're not coming.

Where you are is not your destiny. You haven't reached your limits. You haven't seen your best days.

This is where your faith has to kick in. You should live with expectancy that the new thing is coming. "By faith, I can see the healing that's coming. I can see promotion on its way. I can see my child turning around. I can see myself free from this addiction."

"*Now* it springs forth." Not one day, not in the sweet by and by, but today. *Today*, God is doing a new thing. *Today*, God is making rivers in your desert. *Today*, God is turning your dry places into abundant places. If you'll stay in faith, you're going to see the new thing.

Where you are is not your destiny. You haven't reached your limits. You haven't seen your best days. This new thing is going to spring forth and be something that you've never seen.

The Scripture says, "... *do you not perceive it?*" (v. 19, NIV). It implies that God can be doing it, but there's no sign of it. "Joel, I don't see anything new happening in my life. I'm still struggling, still lonely, still sick; I still have this problem at work." Yes, but what you can't see is the new thing has already sprung forth. It's already in motion. It's on the way. At the right time, it's going to show up. You could see your new thing tomorrow, you could see your breakthrough this week, you could get that scholarship this month, you could see your healing, your promotion, your abundance this year because it has already sprung forth. It's there, just below the surface, ready to breakthrough when the time is right.

When God says He's going to do a new thing, He means it's not going to be like the old thing. It's going to be different. The new thing may not be what you were expecting. It may not happen the way you thought it would. It may not involve the people you thought it would. The circumstances may be different.

Could it be that God is doing a new thing, right now, today, and you don't perceive it because it's not happening the way you thought it would? He is opening a door, but you don't want to go through it because it looks different than what you thought it would. He's bringing people across your path who are divine connections, but they're not who you were expecting. Don't get set in your way. The new thing may not look like what you had in mind but stay open for how God is going to do it. Don't put Him in a box and limit Him to one way. Most of the time, the way we want it done is less than what God has in mind. What He has planned will be much bigger, much better. Trust Him to do it His way. If we're set in how we want it to happen, we can miss perceiving and knowing the new thing that has already sprung forth.

Here's the question: can you perceive it? Do you believe that God's up to something amazing? No more looking in the rearview mirror, start looking forward, start expecting His goodness today. This is a new day. God is doing a new thing in your life.

Declaration

God, this is a new day, and You are doing a new thing. I will keep my eyes open to the unexpected because I know that what You are planning for my life even now is springing forth. It is happening right here, now, today, and soon I will see it come to pass.

Don't Burden Your Blessing

The mistake we make too often is we get in a hurry and try to make things happen in our own timing. This is what the younger son did in the story of the prodigal son. He went to his father and said, *"Give me the portion of goods that falls to me"* (Luke 15:12, NKJV). They were rightfully his; it was his inheritance. But a blessing given at the wrong time is not a blessing.

Something may have your name on it, and you know God has put it in your heart. But if it happens too soon and you're not prepared, that blessing will turn into a burden. For example, say God has a 100-pound blessing for you, but you can only carry

50 pounds. If God gave that 100-pound blessing to you now, it wouldn't be a blessing. It would be a burden because you can't carry it yet. You are still building your spiritual muscles. You are still preparing for your blessing.

Luke 15 continues:

> It wasn't long before the younger son packed his bags and left for a distant country. There, undisciplined and dissipated, he wasted everything he had. After he had gone through all his money, there was a bad famine all through that country and he began to feel it. He signed on with a citizen there who assigned him to his fields to slop the pigs. He was so hungry he would have eaten the corncobs in the pig slop, but no one would give him any. (vv. 13–16, MSG)

The young son was "undisciplined" and "dissipated" (immoral). He hadn't yet fully matured. He got his inheritance too soon. This young man wanted his prepared blessing, but the problem was he was unprepared. He couldn't support the weight of what God had in store. Because it wasn't his right time, he went out and wasted what was given to him.

I used to pray, "God, give me everything in a hurry." Now I've learned to pray, "God, don't give me anything too soon. Don't take me anywhere that I can't handle. Don't open a door that I don't have the grace to walk through. Give me the patience to stay in the waiting room, to develop so I'm ready for what belongs to me."

A good father won't give a good gift at the wrong time. Sometimes God proves His love to us by what He's *not* letting us have. It doesn't mean it's not going to happen; it's just not the right time. He is still preparing us for it. We are growing, developing, gaining experience, learning to trust Him, learning to forgive, learning to be good to those who have wronged us, and practicing being mature enough to receive with a good attitude. The sooner we pass these tests, the sooner God will release the things that belong to us.

Psalm 37:34 says, "*Don't be impatient for the Lord to act! Keep traveling steadily along his pathway and in due season he will honor you with every blessing*" (TLB). Stay faithful while you wait. Don't get impatient, don't complain because it's taking a long time, don't get upset because the door closed, and don't live jealous of others. Travel steady, and honor God. He will give you every blessing!

That means you won't have to make it happen in your own strength. You won't have to manipulate people or try to force doors to open. God will give you the position, give you the spouse, give you the contract, give you the home, give you the ideas, give you the influence. Whatever it is that He has promised you, He will give to you!

Don't fight the wait. You're not falling behind. God has already lined up the blessings He's going to give you. He's already put your name on things bigger and better than you've imagined. Relax and enjoy the wait! Keep traveling steady. Keep trusting Him when you don't see anything happening. Keep honoring God, and He will give you every blessing!

Declaration

God, You don't have to rush to give me my blessings. I will wait patiently and faithfully and steadily because I know that You know better than I do when I am ready to receive it, to handle it, to be successful in it. I am not going to waste my inheritance. At the right time, You will give me every blessing!

Practice Patience

When I was eight years old, at Christmas time, I went with my father to buy a bike for my little sister April. He wanted me to help pick out what I thought she would like. He had me get on different ones to try them out and see if I thought they would fit her. After about a half an hour, we finally picked out her bike. My father said he was going to come back and get it later. In a couple of days, I noticed on our back patio, a large sheet covering the bike we bought her. I went over and was about to pull the sheet back when my father said, "No, Joel, I don't want you to look at it." I said, "Why? I've already seen it." He said, "I just don't want you to." He didn't give me a real reason.

This was about two weeks before Christmas. Every day I asked my father if I could look at the bike. He told me no again and again. I couldn't understand it. What was it going to hurt? Finally, Christmas morning came around. All of us kids slept in the den on Christmas Eve. At six o'clock, we ran and woke our parents up. We opened some gifts under the tree, then my father said, "April, we have another gift out on the patio." We went out, and my father pulled the sheet off. There wasn't just one bike — there were two bikes. One for April and one for me as well. My father had really taken me to the store to find out what I liked!

What if God is not letting you see something now because He wants it to be a surprise. It's not the right time to reveal it, so He's keeping the cover on it. But when it's your time, it's going to surprise you! It's going to be something you never imagined. There are some things He has covered for you right now, but the good news is your time is coming. When He uncovers it, you're going to say, "It was worth the wait!"

Speaking of waiting, did you know that elephants are pregnant for nearly two years? That's right! It takes an average of 22 months for a baby elephant to grow and develop and be ready to come into the world at a whopping 200–300 pounds! Obviously giving birth to multiples is out of the question. Less than one percent of elephant births are twins.

Dogs, on the other hand, give birth after just 63 days of being pregnant. Average litter sizes are five or six puppies. These newborn puppies are so tiny they aren't even measured in pounds, they are measured in ounces or grams! Dogs can give birth up to three times a year, which means that a female dog can have as many as 36 puppies in the time that it takes one elephant baby to come into the world!

Don't get discouraged if what you are waiting for is taking longer than you expected. It may feel like God is hiding it under the covers, but that doesn't mean anything is wrong. It means that there is a surprise under there; it means that what you are about to give birth to is so much bigger than average that it requires more time to come to fruition. You think you are expecting puppies, but God wants to surprise you with an elephant.

My challenge for you is this: don't be impatient for God to act. Don't be frustrated by what's not happening. God is working under the covers while you are in the waiting room. You're being prepared for what God has prepared for you. The reason it's taken longer than you thought is because God wants to surprise you with something better than you thought. You have an elephant in you that He is about to birth. God is about to uncover some things that you didn't see coming. He's going to surprise you with promotion, opportunity, divine connections, favor, and new levels of your destiny.

Declaration

God, I am like a kid on Christmas morning, eagerly awaiting the surprise You have for me. My dreams are like puppies compared to the elephant You have in mind for me. I will relax and practice patience while I wait for the bigger, better surprise You have for me!

Prepared Blessings

When God laid out the plan for your life, He lined up the right people, the right breaks, and the right opportunities. He has blessings that have your name on them. There's promotion, contracts, a business, a spouse, healing, restoration, and He's already destined them to be yours. If you'll stay in faith and keep honoring God, at the right time you'll come into what already belongs to you. It's a prepared blessing.

That's what happened way back with Adam and Eve. In the book of Genesis, it talks about how, in the first five days of Creation, God created the Heavens, the earth, the sky, the land, and the water. When He finished the big things, He didn't stop there. He got down to the small things, the details. He planted a garden and put beautiful flowers in it, and luscious fruit. He designed rivers to flow through it. He put precious treasures in the ground: onyx, gold, and silver. He went to great lengths to make sure it was exactly what He wanted, down to the smallest details. When He finally put the last touches on this magnificent garden, the Scripture says He took Adam, whom He had just breathed life into, and put Him in the garden (see Genesis 2:15).

He's working behind the scenes right now, arranging things in your favor.

Adam came into a prepared blessing, something that God had already finished for him. He didn't get there and have to struggle. There was provision everywhere he looked. Everything he needed to live a victorious, abundant life was right there in the garden. God had specifically prepared it for him. In the same way, God has some prepared blessings in store for you. He's working behind the scenes right now, arranging things in your favor, getting it all perfectly in place. At the right time, He's going to bring you into your garden, into what He's already finished for you. You couldn't have made it happen on your own, you didn't deserve it, you didn't earn it — it's just the goodness of God bringing you into a prepared blessing.

When I was twenty-two years old, I walked into a jewelry store and met Victoria for the first time. She was a prepared blessing. I looked up and said, "God, you did good." There are thousands of jewelry stores in a big city like Houston that I could have gone into, but God controls the whole universe. He knows how to bring you into your garden. He said in effect, "Joel, I've got something finished for you. I've got a prepared blessing that I'm ready to bring you into." God directed my steps. I met Victoria that day, and my life has never been the same.

Don't get discouraged. You may not see anything happening, but God is at work, getting your garden prepared. He is putting in the right resources, lining up the right people, arranging things in your favor. When it's in full bloom, just like He wants it, He's going to bring you into it. Suddenly you'll be promoted, you'll get that contract, you'll move into the new house, and the problem will turn around. When you come into your garden, it's going to be bigger, better, and more rewarding than you ever dreamed.

God said in Deuteronomy 8:7–9,

> *For the Lord your God is bringing you into a good land, a land of brooks of water, of fountains and springs, that flow out of valleys and hills; a land of wheat and barley, of vines*

*and fig trees and pomegranates, a land of olive
oil and honey; a land in which you will eat
bread without scarcity, in which you will lack
nothing.* (NKJV)

Notice in the garden God is preparing for you,
there will be no shortage: no shortage of opportunity, no shortage of resources, no shortage of
creativity, friendships, joy, or peace. In this garden
you will not lack any good thing. That's God's
dream for your life — to bring you into a garden
of abundance, a garden filled with favor, opportunity, good health, and great relationships. It is your
prepared blessing.

Declaration

God, I want to thank You that I'm coming into my
garden. You are preparing blessings for me, places
of no shortage and no lack — a good land where
my gifts and talents will flourish into fullness and
I'll live healthy, whole and free.

Blessings Stored Up

Psalm 31:19 says, "*Oh, how great is your goodness to those who publicly declare that you will rescue them. For you have stored up great blessings for those who trust and reverence you*" (TLB).

God has blessings stored up for you simply because you trust in Him. There are businesses stored up that God is about to release. There is promotion stored up; it has your name on it. There's a new house stored up, a baby stored up, a husband stored up, healing stored up, and because you love the Lord God, He is about to release what He has prepared for you. You're not going to have to go find the blessings — the blessings are going to find you. Something is tracking you down right now. It's not defeat, not lack, not self-pity. Instead, favor is looking for you, promotion is looking for you, healing is looking for you, that contract is looking for you. You're about to see something that you've never seen before — the blessings that God has stored up for you.

I have a friend who was planning to build a new sanctuary. It was going to cost about $40 million. He was raising the funds and starting to draw up the plans. One day, out of the blue, the mayor called him and told him there was a group that built a huge casino, but before they moved in, they went bankrupt. They had over 40 acres of parking, a building that could fit four football fields inside, and it was just a few miles from his current church. The mayor asked if he was interested in purchasing it. The pastor thought it would be at least $50 million. It was huge, first class — way more than the facility he was planning on building. The mayor said, "You can have it for less than $2 million." A man who owned a production company got word of the sale. He said to my friend, "I've got a big screen that's used for concerts and sporting events. It's over a 150 feet long. It cost $3 million new, but I'll sell it to you for $50,000." Things began to fall into place. Instead of having to build their own facility, God dropped a much bigger and better facility into their hands. That was a blessing stored up — something that God had already prepared, and at the right time God released it.

If you could see what God has stored up for you, the blessings He has prepared for you, the people you're going to meet, the places you're going to go, the good breaks that are going to find you, it would boggle your mind. You're going to see the surpassing greatness of God's favor as He reveals to you the blessings He has stored up.

Too often we look at our circumstances and come up with excuses as to why it's not going to happen: "Joel, I don't have the training, the talent, the connections. I'm the wrong nationality. I'm too short. I'll never come into my blessing." Lucky for us, God is not limited by our circumstances, by what family we come from, by who's against us. When God breathed His life into you, He placed a blessing on you that overrides anything that's trying to hold you back. The blessing God has for you cannot be stopped by bad breaks, by people, or by injustice, because God has already stored it up for you. God has the final say. Of the blessings He has prepared for you, He has every intention of bringing you into.

The Bible tells us not to store up treasures on earth (Matthew 6:19). We don't have to become hoarders of God's treasure because He already has a stockpile of blessings stored up for each one of us. We can focus on building the Kingdom of Heaven because He has already taken care of building up for us our blessings here on earth. Our job is to keep trusting Him, to keep praising Him while we wait, to keep declaring that the promises of God are stored up for us and are about to be released into our lives. The blessings He has stored up for us are so much bigger and better than earthly things.

Declaration

God, You are the Creator of all things, and You have blessings stored up for me. I am enjoying the wait because I know that You are good and what You have in store is beyond my wildest imagination!

The Blessing That Belongs to You

When we see good things happen to other people, we might be tempted to worry that their blessing is going to keep God from doing something good for us, as if they're using up all of God's favor. But I want you to see that the blessing that belongs to you will be your blessing. Nobody can take it.

In the Scripture, we see David as a powerful king, a great man, one of the heroes of faith, but David didn't come from a royal family. He hadn't been trained to take the throne, raised in wealth and influence. His family was very poor. He was the eighth son of a man named Jesse. His brothers were all involved in the army and had prestigious positions, but David's job was to take care of his father's sheep. He was looked down upon, seen as secondary. It didn't look like he had much of a future outside of the sheep fields. But just because people write you off, doesn't mean God writes you off. Circumstances may look like you are stuck, and you'll never get out, but that doesn't change what God has prepared for you. The blessing God put on you will override any curse, any setback, any lack. What God has prepared for you is not affected by people or circumstances. The blessing that belongs to you is your destiny.

One day the prophet Samuel came to Jesse's house to anoint one of his sons as the next king of Israel. Seven of these sons were lined up in the house. Jesse was so proud. Samuel went down the row, one by one. He turned the bottle over to pour the oil out to anoint the first son, but the oil wouldn't flow. He thought, "It's not this one." He moved on to the second son. He tried to pour it out, but the oil wouldn't flow. He moved to the next one — same thing — then the next and the next. He went through all seven sons. Samuel was confused. He knew God had spoken to him that he was to anoint a son of Jesse, but the oil wouldn't flow. He said to Jesse, "God hasn't chosen any of these. Is this it?

Are there no more sons?" (see 1 Samuel 16:10–11). Jesse said, "Well I do have one other son, but I'm sure it's not him. He's the youngest, the runt; he's out tending sheep." Samuel said, "Bring him in." David was brought to stand before Samuel, and this time, when Samuel poured the oil, it began to flow and flow. He knew right then David was the next king.

Here's the point: you don't have to worry about somebody else getting your blessing. The oil that's prepared for you will not flow out to anyone else. When Samuel tried to anoint the other sons, the oil defied gravity. It would not flow. I can see Samuel turning the bottle over, hitting the top, but the oil would not come out until it recognized the right person that was supposed to be blessed. When it's your time to be blessed, nobody can take your blessing. The blessing that's prepared for you will not flow out to anyone else. That's why you can relax and stay in peace, knowing that God's got you covered. Nobody is going to get what belongs to you.

You may think, "My coworker got the promotion that I deserved; my sister got the husband I deserved; my friend wrote the book that I should have written; my neighbor has the child I've always wanted." In reality, if you didn't get it, it wasn't supposed to be yours. Your oil is not going to flow for somebody else. The blessing that belongs to you will be your blessing.

Here's the key: you can pray for others to be blessed because their blessing has no bearing on yours. God is infinite in wisdom and grace and love. He can bless your neighbor and your sister and your friend and still have enough to bless you too. And He not only blesses you, but He blesses you with the perfect blessing that belongs to only you.

Declaration

God, I am perfectly at peace because I know that the blessing You have for me is not in any way affected by the blessing You have for anyone else. Thank You for blessing my family, my friends, my neighbors, my enemies, and me.

A Place of Abundance

The Scripture tells of Elijah living in a certain city when God said to him, "*Get away from here and turn eastward, and turn eastward, and hide by the Brook Cherith, which flows into the Jordan. And it will be that you shall drink from the brook, and I have command-ed the ravens to feed you there*" (1 Kings 17:3–4, NKJV). Elijah obeyed. He moved where God commanded. He went every day to the brook to drink, and every day the ravens would come and feed him.

It is important to note that Elijah didn't have to find the ravens. He just had to get where God wanted him to be, and the ravens found him. In the same way, there is a place where God has commanded you to be blessed. The ravens are already there. Your provision, your favor, your increase are waiting on you. The question is, will you do what's required? Elijah could have said, "God, I don't want to leave this place; I like it here. I'm comfortable; my friends are here." The thing is, if he would have stayed, he would have missed where he was commanded to be blessed. He could have survived, he could have endured; but if you want to see God's best, you've got to be willing to do what you know God is asking you to do and go where God is asking you to go.

Maybe deep down you know you're supposed to get away from some friends who are a bad influence. They are dragging you down, causing you to be negative, and to compromise. As long as you stay there, you're going to miss your place of abundance. God has something more for you. He has favor, increase, and provision for you, but you've got to be willing to make the changes He asks of you. "Well, Joel, if I do that, I'll be lonely. I won't have any friends." Yes, you may be lonely for a season, but God will always bring you new friends; He'll bring you better friends. It may be difficult for a time, but before long, you'll come into that place of abundance. The ravens will be there. Greater joy, greater fulfilment, and new relationships will be there.

It may not be leaving friends or moving physically that God is asking of you. It may be a change in your mind. Maybe God is calling you to leave the negative thoughts, the worry, the anxiety, the offense, the resentment, or the anger behind. Whatever it is, God has a place of abundance for you — a place where He's commanded you to be blessed, but you've got to do your part and leave what He's asking you to leave. It will probably mean you have to get out of your comfort zone and take a step of faith, but you can't play it safe all your life and expect to reach your highest potential.

At one point in Elijah's story, the ravens quit coming to the brook — not because God was mad at Elijah, but because He was ready to send Elijah somewhere new. Your place of abundance can move! God told Elijah, "*Arise, go to Zarephath, which belongs to Sidon, and dwell there. See, I have commanded a widow there to provide for you*" (1 Kings 17:9, NKJV). His place of blessing moved. If he would have been set in his ways and thought, "I know God sent me here to the brook; these ravens have fed me for years. I am not leaving," he would have missed the new thing God wanted to do.

For 17 years I was happy, fulfilled, and seeing God's favor behind the scenes at the church, but when my father died, I could hear God whispering, "Joel, I'm moving you from behind the scenes to out in front of the people." It was uncomfortable. I had to stretch. But I took that step of faith and walked into a new season of favor, influence, and abundance.

Don't hold on to the old when you know God is leading you somewhere new. Get out of your comfort zone. God has a place of abundance, and He is calling you to step into it.

Declaration

God, I will follow You into a place of abundance. When You call me to move, I'll move. When You call me to stay, I'll stay. I will not bow down to fear. I am ready for something new!

Your Time to Reign

Psalm 8:5 says that God has "crowned" us with favor. He used the word "crown" to let us know we're supposed to reign. If anything negative has been reigning over you, there's about to be a shift — a change in authority. You're about to reign over what's been reigning over you.

Second Chronicles 23 tells the story of a boy named Joash. When Joash was a baby, his uncle, the king of Judah was killed. One of the king's sons should have taken the throne, but the king's mother, Athaliah, decided she wanted to be the queen, so she had all of her children and grandchildren killed. She was then the next rightful heir to the throne. Someone heard what she was doing and took baby Joash, Athaliah's grandson, to the temple and kept him safe. He was the only member of the royal family to survive.

The priest in the temple at the time was named Jehoiada. He and his wife took care of little Joash, keeping him hidden, knowing he was destined to take the throne. When Joash was seven years old, Johoiada went to five different army captains: "*Jehoiada said to them, 'Here is the king's son! The time has come for him to reign! The LORD has promised that a descendant of David will be our king'*" (2 Chronicles 23:3, NLT). It didn't seem like he was ready to reign; he was only seven years old. He didn't have the training, the experience, the size, or the wisdom. Nevertheless, Jehoiada showed up and said, "It's time."

Maybe you've had some bad breaks, you weren't raised in a healthy environment, you feel like you're at a disadvantage, you've been overlooked, and pushed down. That would keep most people in defeat, living a mediocre life, but not you. You're a king's son. You're a king's daughter. You have an advantage. There is a favor on your life, a blessing that will lift you up when life tries to push you down, an anointing to excel when you should be limited, to rise higher when you should be stuck, to defeat the odds, to outlast the opposition. Like little Joash, it's your time to reign!

Second Chronicles 24:1–2 says, "*Joash was seven years old when he became king, and he reigned in Jerusalem forty years... Joash did what was right in the eyes of the LORD all the years of Jehoiada the priest*" (NIV). I believe one reason God crowned Joash king at such an early age is God knew He could trust him. He knew he would do what was right. Like his ancestor David, Joash had a heart after God and wanted to please Him. Joash wasn't perfect. Like David, he made mistakes, but he had a desire to honor God.

When God can trust you, when He knows He can count on you to honor him, to handle the influence and the resources the right way, then there's no limit to where God will take you. You don't have to be perfect; we all make mistakes. It's not so much about your performance; it's about your heart.

The Most High God, the Creator of the Universe, is fighting for you.

Whatever has been reigning over you — the dysfunction, the lack, the sickness — this is a new day. There's about to be a turnaround. It's your time to reign. You haven't missed your chance. You haven't made too many mistakes. Your obstacles are not too big. You can get your passion back. You can get your fire back. You wouldn't be reading this if God wasn't about to do something unusual, something unprecedented. The reason the enemy is fighting you is because there's a calling on your life. There is an assignment for you to fulfill. The fact that you have forces trying to stop you is a sign that you have an awesome destiny. The enemy wouldn't be fooling with you if you weren't a threat. The good news is the forces that are for you are greater than the forces that are against you. You're not fighting by yourself. The Most High God, the Creator of the Universe, is fighting for you. You're on the verge of seeing favor that you've never seen. It's your time to reign!

Declaration

God, I believe that chains are being broken right now. You are pushing back forces of darkness right now. That thing that has tried to take my life is no longer in charge. There's been a power shift. It's my time to reign!

Don't be impatient for the Lord to act! Keep traveling steadily along his pathway and in due season he will honor you with every blessing . . .

Psalm 37:34, TLB

Books by Joel Osteen